50 Christian Assemblies
for Primary Schools

50 Christian Assemblies for Primary Schools

Chris Nicholls

50 CHRISTIAN ASSEMBLIES FOR PRIMARY SCHOOLS
Published by David C. Cook
Kingsway Communications Ltd
Lottbridge Drove, Eastbourne BN23 6NT, England
books@kingsway.co.uk

David C. Cook
4050 Lee Vance View, Colorado Springs, CO 80918 U.S.A.

David C. Cook Distribution Canada
55 Woodslee Avenue, Paris, Ontario, Canada N3L 3E5

David C. Cook and the graphic circle C logo
are registered trademarks of Cook Communications Ministries.

The website addresses recommended throughout this book are
offered as a resource to you. Third-party websites are not intended in
any way to be or imply an endorsement on the part of David C. Cook,
nor do we vouch for their content.

ISBN 978 1 842913 24 6

Designed by PinnacleCreative.co.uk
Top Photo: © 2006 BonnieJ I Dreamstime.com

Printed in the USA
First Edition 2007

1 2 3 4 5 6 7 8 9 10

CONTENTS

Note

Due to format constraints, the artwork in this book has been reduced in size.
Those marked 'pdf available' can also be found at www.canicholls.com

ACKNOWLEDGEMENTS

There are so many people to whom I owe a great deal with regard to my ministry that it is difficult to know where to begin and where to end. But perhaps Open Air Campaigners is a good place to start, and I would like to dedicate this book to them. I joined OAC in 1992 and stayed with them as Director of the Eastbourne branch for eight years. OAC are an international and interdenominational faith mission dedicated to taking the gospel of Jesus Christ to people where they are, including streets, shopping precincts, parks, seafronts, housing estates, places of work, prisons, colleges and schools. It was during my time with OAC that I was able to rub shoulders with incredible communicators who helped me develop a successful schools and open-air ministry.

Special thanks go to David and Alice Fanstone, Derek and Mavis Heyman, and the many other close friends I made during my time with OAC. Derek was the person who introduced me to street preaching with the sketch-board and also to the art of communicating the gospel to children in a way that is fun and understandable to them.

Over the years members of OAC would come and go, and for this reason I have only been able to mention a few. However, they all know who they are, and it is them that I thank and to whom I will always be indebted. It's because of them that this book has been possible. OAC people are a rare breed that can come up with creative ways of communicating the gospel of Jesus Christ – and then graciously give their ideas away to be used by others in the building of God's Kingdom. This book is full of their thoughts intermingled with mine, and I know they would wish to join me in asking you to make these talks your own and, in doing so, to make Christ known.

A big thank you has to go to family friend Jeanette Walter. Jeanette, thank you so much, not just for contributing some of the talks but also for spending many hours going over my drafts and making them intelligible!

My thanks to Ben Ecclestone for illustrating the introductory chapters, and to James Hammond for the illustrations to the Zacchaeus talk ('Small Man, Big Change. . .') and the Shadrach, Meshach and Abednego talk ('Be Cool!'). The illustrations to the Naaman talk ('Skinny Dipping') were inspired by original drawings by Jonathan David Inc.,1997. All other illustrations are by yours truly – so thank you to me too!

Heartfelt thanks must of course go to my church, Frenchgate Christian Fellowship, and to everyone who has supported my ministry and encouraged me over the years. My dear friends Dr John Caroe and his wife Linda were instrumental in the early days in helping me understand the psychology of working with young children, knowledge that was also to prove invaluable when starting my entertainment business.

And finally, to my wife Jean, daughters Emilie and Jenny and their husbands Andrew and Gareth, not forgetting our two fantastic grandchildren Joshua and Nathan: thank you for being not only a wonderful family but also my friends.

INTRODUCTION

LET ME ENTERTAIN YOU

I am a professional children's entertainer who came to realise that when taking assemblies I was using the same skills I use when entertaining children. (These aren't the same skills you need in the classroom.) So the outlines in this book all reflect my skill base and my personality – I know of no other way of presenting them – but it is important that when you use one of these talks, you make it your own – just as I do with ideas given to me by other people. To be successful in engaging with children, I would encourage you to use your own words and adapt these outlines to suit your own style.

The talks are also informed by my faith and so, before going any further, it may be useful to address the following three questions.

1. WHAT IS A CHRISTIAN ASSEMBLY?

As a Bible-believing Christian, I should like to suggest the following definition:

> A Christian assembly is one that refers to any issue as long as the focal point, through Scripture, is Christ.

You will notice that the majority of the outlines in this book contain some reference to the gospel message. However, I do not repeat this every time I talk to the same group of children, as I do not want them to become 'gospel-hardened'. It is for you to decide whether to refer to the cross in any particular assembly and, if so, in how much depth.

It is often assumed that it's enough just to deal with moral issues in a Christian assembly, such as being kind to others. This is a good thing to discuss, but I would not consider it to be a Christian assembly. It could equally well be a

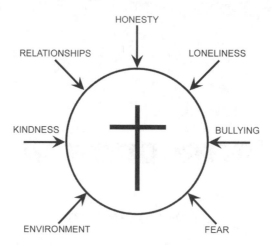

Muslim assembly, a Hindu assembly or even a secular assembly. Christians don't have the monopoly on virtue! However, as some schools will want to record the values they are addressing in their assembly times, all of the outlines in this book are cross-indexed by value as well as Bible passage.

The problem with making assemblies 'acceptable' to everyone is that you have to start diluting Christianity. And if Christianity is diluted to the point where it becomes universally acceptable, it is no longer Christianity.

It seems to me important to keep in mind each individual child's spiritual search for meaning. We shouldn't be trying to sell Christianity to the children and, in fact, we couldn't do that even if we tried. In any case, to attempt to do so would be contravening educational guidelines, not to mention breaking the law. You will notice that I frequently qualify statements of Christian faith with the words, 'This is what the Bible teaches and what Christians believe.' In this way you are staying within the guidelines and the law, but at the same time allowing the Holy Spirit to do what you cannot.

I strongly feel that in a Christian assembly we should be exposing children to *real Christianity* (i.e. how Christians see it) so that they can explore it for themselves and make up their own minds – *whether or not we ourselves are Christians*. Otherwise we are not giving them the whole picture.

2. WHAT IS WORSHIP?

My own interpretation of worship is: *a heartfelt response of love and reverence towards God.* It can take place while listening to a talk, singing, praying, reflecting, looking at creation, being creative or serving others. On the other hand, simply reflecting on the merits of being kind to others, while it would be a good exercise, would not in my opinion constitute Christian worship.

By definition, worship cannot be enforced. It must be voluntary. It is important to give children the freedom to respond in a variety of ways, even if it's simply to observe and appreciate that worship is important to Christians.

3. WHAT DO CHRISTIANS BELIEVE?

All the talks in this book are based on the credo of Bible-believing Christians. For anyone unfamiliar with this, it may be helpful to summarise it here.

- Man was created for a relationship with God, and given free will so that the relationship would be voluntary and meaningful.
- Free will has led man into sin, which separates us from God who is by nature perfect.
- God, in the person of Jesus, became a man in order to live the only perfect human life and so became the perfect sacrifice for the sins of human beings by his death on the cross. He then, being also God, rose from the dead.
- If anyone
    - accepts that Jesus died for them
    - sincerely wants to change and turn away from their old life
    - and trusts their life to Jesus
  then God will
    - forgive that person
    - come to live in that person by his Holy Spirit
    - work in their life to change them
    - and give them eternal life with himself
  Christians also believe that
    - the gospels are historical accounts
    - the Old Testament prophecies were actually fulfilled in history, not just on paper
    - and the whole of Scripture is inspired by God and can be read on many levels; that it contains living metaphors, not just literary ones

When Christians trust Jesus, they are not entrusting their lives to a myth! Children should be aware of that, shouldn't they?

CREATING ATMOSPHERE

Music is very powerful. It affects people's mood. It can switch people on, and it can switch people off. When some railway stations were having a problem with large groups of youths hanging around, they hit on the idea of playing Delius over the PA system. And – guess what – it worked! The music, which many people like, repelled the youngsters.

It's something to be aware of if you intend to use music in your assembly, whether you're going for classical or modern. If you choose something simply because you like it, but the children are sitting there being switched off or even repelled, then you've got an uphill struggle to get them back when you begin your talk. You can give yourself a head start with music that children relate to.

Have you noticed how some adults listen to a speaker without any visible reaction? They gaze into space or even have their eyes closed. They're interested, but they're not going to show it! Very off-putting for the speaker!

So if you have any colleagues who are going to be sitting round the edge of the assembly, ask them beforehand to *react* to your presentation – to look at you and react in all the right places – because the children will notice this out of the corner of their eye, and it will encourage an atmosphere of response in them. And that will help you. It will 'oil the wheels' of your assembly.

A word about that destroyer of atmosphere – notices! You come into an assembly with something positive you want the children to go away with. But there's a problem because some of the children have been climbing on the toilet roof again, and if you're a teacher you've got to give out a stern notice about it. Psychologists say it takes ten positives to outweigh one negative. So how do you get round the problem? Well, it would certainly help you in creating the right atmosphere for your act of worship if the supervision, discipline and notices were looked after by someone other than yourself. That way the waters don't get muddied and the act of worship remains 'special'.

OVERCOMING THE CRINGE FACTOR

You will need to find a way of holding the attention of a large number of children as you deliver your talk and present your assembly. Children are often entertained by things we find ridiculous. So we need to be prepared to lose our inhibitions!

- You only get back from your audience the degree of enthusiasm that you put into it. Your audience is a mirror – they reflect back what they see. If you are enthusiastic, they will be too.
- If you take a chance and find it works, your confidence takes over from your self-consciousness. When I first started this work, someone said I ought to get a puppet. I got one, started practising in front of the mirror, and thought, 'Nobody in their right mind is going to buy this!' But in schools it was an instant success. If I hadn't taken the chance, I'd have missed out on a winner.
- Be prepared to fail. For example, I had an idea for the start of a puppet routine, where before the puppet, Jimmy, came out of his case he would blow his nose. So I opened the case and Jimmy said, 'I want to blow my nose,' and I made the funny noise. Nobody laughed! I thought about it and realised I hadn't cued the children properly. Next time Jimmy said, 'I'm not ready!' we had a conversation: 'Why aren't you ready?' 'I want to blow my nose!' 'He wants to blow his nose, boys and girls!' 'Go on then *Jimmy*, blow your nose!' Then when I made the noise, everyone fell about laughing.

So remember – failure is never final. You learn more from your mistakes than you do from your successes. And the *fear* of failure will evaporate if you put into practice the techniques in this book – because you can be confident that they work.

Of course assemblies are easier for extroverts – and you may be an introvert. But introverts can function in an extrovert way quite successfully for short periods of time. Just like if you're right-handed, you can train yourself to write a few sentences fairly well with your left hand. But if you had to write left-handed all day long, you'd be worn out.

So first define your character. Don't try to imitate someone else, however much you admire them. Develop your own unique style. The character you project should be the best side of your personality. When you're driving your car up a hill and you want more power, you don't change your car – you change gear. In an assembly you need to change gear too. You need to *exaggerate your natural self*.

ROUNDING THEM UP

You may walk out in front of the sea of faces in fear and trepidation, saying to yourself, 'I'll just look at it as an extended class.' This would be a big mistake. Large groups are very different from small ones, and you need to look on them as an audience. To a group you give a talk; to an audience you give a performance.

Children will not listen attentively to a speaker who does not look at them while he or she is talking. Eye contact is probably the most effective means of non-verbal communication there is. When you look directly at your listeners, you pick up clues that tell you whether they understand what you are saying, and whether they are interested. You can then adjust accordingly.

Also, if you look a child in the eye, he or she will feel that you want to talk to them personally. The children are made to feel important and it builds a relationship between you and them. If you show interest in them, they will show interest in you. It makes them feel accountable to you; they'll be wondering what you are thinking about them.

BUT HOW CAN YOU MAKE EYE CONTACT WITH THREE OR FOUR HUNDRED CHILDREN?

At the beginning, pick out a few key children around the hall who look interested. Address your remarks to them, in turn, as though what you are saying is just for that child. Look them straight in the eye. Because of the dilution of distance (more about that in the next section) the children sitting on either side and just behind and in front of the key child, will think you are looking at them. So when you look at one child, at least five will think you are looking exclusively at them! And they will start to look more interested.

Next time, look generally at that group of five, and the circle of children around them will think you are looking at them. So every time your eyes come back to that area of the hall, the circle of interested faces gets bigger – until the circles overlap. You have now made every child in the hall think you are watching them.

NOW YOU'VE GOT THEIR ATTENTION, DON'T LOSE IT

Move about – but as you move, maintain eye contact. Keep facing the children as much as possible. Don't leave the front. If you approach one particular child and hold a conversation with him/her, you've then got to 'round everyone up' with your eye contact exercise all over again.

It's easy enough to get children excited, but you also have to be able to bring them down again. I can't stress enough the importance of keeping control (but without turning into Mr or Ms Grumpy!) I have a technique which works every time. I introduce it at the start of an assembly, especially when I am new to a school, or at the beginning of the academic year when new children are present. It goes like this:

> We like to have fun, don't we girls and boys? But there are times when we have to be serious as well. So – if you see me fold my arms and say the word 'ship-shape', it means that I want you all to be sitting up straight, facing the front and paying attention. Let's have a practice. Talk to the person next to you and tell them what you had for breakfast this morning. But when you hear me say the word 'ship-shape', I want you to stop.

The children enjoy responding to this code word, which is far more user-friendly than the 'be quiet' telling-off type of command. In fact, children often refer to me as 'Mr Ship-Shape'!

In a hall full of children, there may be times when a particular child, for whatever reason, becomes disruptive. Teachers sitting round the edge are good at policing the children's behaviour, but it is your responsibility to be aware of what is going on in all parts of the hall at all times, and to be ready to respond accordingly.

- If you need a volunteer, choose the disruptive child to help you. This might seem like rewarding bad behaviour, but it's quite possible that the child is craving attention. By giving him or her something useful to do, you are increasing that child's self-esteem and at the same time dealing effectively with the disruption.
- If you don't need a volunteer, then speak directly to the child in a manner that is firm but not angry, and tell him or her to go and sit with a teacher.

Having said that, disruption is rare in assemblies that engage the children's imagination and keep their attention – such as those in this book!

THE DILUTION OF DISTANCE

In an assembly hall, the children are separated from you by a lot more distance than in a classroom. That distance dilutes the clarity of your speech and your gestures. You need to correct that dilution of distance, accentuating everything you do so that it looks natural by the time it gets to the children.

Your normal voice and movements will not seem natural in an assembly setting; they will seem weak. If you want to appear natural, you have to exaggerate.

Here are five tools to help you:

1. **Pitch** – the movement of your voice up and down the scale. People who speak in monopitch come across as boring. If you watch television on Saturday and see an interview with a sports personality, you'll probably notice a big difference between the interviewer who has been trained to speak in an interesting way, and the sports personality who hasn't!

   Practise going down in pitch when you go up in force or volume. It will stop you sounding hysterical.

2. **Pace** – the rate at which you speak. Your speech in general should be slowed down. You'll notice that if you ask a child who's a competent reader to read in an assembly, they'll probably do it at their natural speed – and it's very difficult to follow. The distance dilutes the clarity.

   You can emphasise points by changing your rate of delivery. The secret lies in the contrast. When you come to a major point, slow down so that the children will appreciate its importance. Phrases spoken very slowly stand out because they are in strong contrast to what surrounds them. For example:

> 'Simon Peter had gone through a terrible time – all – because – he'd – lied.'

3. **Punch** – which doesn't mean shouting! Project your voice by imagining you are speaking to the back row. But don't shout. Shouting distorts your face and hurts your throat.

   Of course there should be variations in volume to emphasise a single word or a whole idea. Dropping your voice to a near whisper can put an idea into italics as effectively as saying it loudly, because intensity can be as effective as volume. For example:

> 'I don't know what you're talking about!' *Just then, the cock crowed.*

Maintaining the same volume throughout a talk is just as monotonous as monopitch or monopace.

4. **Pauses**. Don't be afraid of silence. Pauses serve as punctuation marks. They give the children a brief opportunity to think, feel and respond.

   The first word or phrase after a pause will stand out from what has preceded it. For example:

> *Just then – (PAUSE) – the cock crowed.*

To emphasise a word, you can pause both before and after it. A pause before the climax of a story increases suspense.

   Many speakers avoid silence. They are afraid the audience will assume they have forgotten what they want to say. But your audience won't think that, as long as you continue your eye contact with them.

5. **Gestures**. Use spontaneous gestures, but make them larger, more forceful and more deliberate than in normal conversation. Gestures should be:

   - **Definite**. A half-hearted gesture communicates nothing positive. If you look uneasy, the children will empathise with that and feel uncomfortable too. Remember, your audience is a reflection of yourself.
   - **Varied**. Undue repetition of a gesture is irritating. (It's worth mentioning here that any kind of fidgeting is extremely off-putting – continually clicking a biro, fiddling with the change in your pocket, rubbing your

nose and so on!) Apparently we can produce 700,000 distinct elementary signs. So experiment with your gestures!

- **Properly timed**. The gesture should either accompany or precede the word or phrase. If it follows, it may look ridiculous. This also applies to other illustrations such as putting up words or pictures on a sketch-board or screen. Ideally the visual illustration needs to come before the word or words to which it refers.

Gestures are good because they

- hold attention
- give the speaker confidence
- help to make the assembly visual
- promote empathy

So – be animated and be larger-than-life!

STAGE FRIGHT

Don't worry about it – it's a function of the adrenal glands! Adrenaline can give you super-human abilities. For example, when you're scared you can run much faster than normal.

But there are five very predictable side-effects of adrenaline:

- Increased heart rate
- Sweaty palms

- Butterflies in your tummy
- Dry mouth
- Feeling of anxiety

These side-effects are *good* because they show you that the mechanism is working well, preparing you to be super-human! So you should be encouraged by the symptoms – be more worried if you *don't* get them!

Once you look at stage fright in this way, it won't overwhelm you.

STORYTELLING

You stand up in front of the children, and even before you've opened your mouth you have a problem to solve. Because *you* know the point you want to make; it's there in your mind and you're already at Point B. But the children don't know; they're still at Point A. So there's a gap between you.

How do you get the children from Point A to Point B? You need to build a bridge. All effective communication builds a bridge between the speaker and the listener. But it's important to remember to *start building from the other side* – from where the children are at, not from where you are at.

For example, if you start by saying something of interest to you – 'Boys and girls, this morning I was driving to school and my fan-belt broke!' – it won't interest them that much and they may not know what a fan-belt is anyway. And, if they're not interested within the first minute, they will probably switch off for the rest of the talk.

But if you say, 'Boys and girls, at the weekend I watched *The X Factor*' (or some other current TV programme that appeals to children) – and then make a comment about it that leads into your talk, they'll be all ears. Because you're starting from where they are at, they'll step onto your bridge.

On your bridge there should also be lights at intervals to guide the children across. These lights are illustrations and explanations that are relevant to them. This way, by the end of your talk, they will have arrived where you are at Point B, and will appreciate the point you are making.

Telling a story is a bit like serving up a meal. You can dish the food onto the plate all in one heap, or you can take the same food and arrange it attractively like they do in the better class of restaurant. If you split a story up into three or four sections, each with its own application, you will:

- make it more appetising
- be able to develop your point in three or four different ways
- maintain the children's attention over a longer period of time

During narrative and illustration the children's attention is likely to be high, but during application their attention is likely to fall. If you leave all your application to the end, the children will realise the story is over and switch off. If you're telling a Bible story, there are lots of children's books of Bible stories available. Choose a story and a version that grabs your attention – one that will be easy for you to bring alive. Try to make it your own, rather than sticking rigidly to other people's words and pictures.

For infants, I feel the story should be no longer than ten minutes; for juniors, no longer than 15 minutes.

Keep it as simple as possible because complexities will get in the way of your main point. But don't be misleading: you can omit parts of a story – but don't change the Bible facts.

Act out your story wherever possible, putting on different voices, using facial expressions and doing the actions. And don't be afraid to use artistic licence to bring the story alive. Before relating the story of Zacchaeus I wanted to convey how mean he was, so I said:

Zacchaeus was very greedy and he didn't like to share! In fact he was so greedy, if he'd had a bag of toffees when he was at school, he would have been able to unwrap a toffee in his pocket with one hand and put it in his mouth with no one seeing.

Remember to make the story visual. Seeing makes a far greater impact on most people than hearing. Eighty per cent of children remember best what they see, whereas only twenty per cent remember best what they hear.

Finally, we all know the importance of dressing up or down for the occasion. It's just as important to make our language appropriate for the occasion. C. S. Lewis was good at doing this. He could write for academics, he could write for children, and he could also write for popular adult consumption. He was a brilliant communicator.

Obviously, language and delivery style is an individual thing and you must be true to your own personality. No two people using a particular talk in this book will put it over in quite the same way. You need to make the talk your own.

Here are some additional suggestions that you may find helpful when putting together a talk from scratch:

- Think in terms of making *one main point* in your talk, although a few supplementary observations can often be successfully incorporated.
- Start with an outline so that your talk doesn't become shapeless.
- Write out what you are going to say. This helps to eliminate waffle. Then reduce it down to notes which will prompt you. Don't read your talk – this kills the lively sense of communication, and don't memorise your talk word-for-word – this kills spontaneity.
- Keep sentences short. Keep sentence structure simple. One thought per sentence.
- Use simple words. Use a short or familiar word unless a longer one is absolutely necessary. For example, instead of 'they were reconciled', say 'they were friends again'. This is good practice when communicating to people of any age. If your listeners have to stop and think about the meaning of a word, they will lose track of what you are saying.
- Use questions to invite the children to think about what you are saying while you are saying it. This is a form of silent audience participation. For example, 'I wonder if you've ever felt that no one understands you?'
- Be vivid. Use evocative words. For instance, if I talk about biting into a lemon, something happens inside your mouth, doesn't it? If you can get the children to connect a feeling they know about with the point you are putting over, they are more likely to remember it.
- Use exact and concrete language which paints pictures in the mind. It is better to say 'oranges, apples and bananas' rather than just 'fruit'.
- Think in pictures. Use illustrations. Use similes and metaphors.

- Let nouns and verbs carry your meaning. Adjectives and adverbs are usually used to try and enliven weak words. So instead of 'he went quickly', say 'he hurried' or 'he ran' or 'he raced'.
- Eliminate 'very' where possible. Instead of 'very hot', say 'steaming' or 'boiling' – or just say 'hot' with tremendous emphasis and appropriate body language!
- Avoid passive verbs. Instead of 'a good time was had by all', say 'they all enjoyed themselves'.
- Read good children's literature out loud. This will impress appropriate picture-making language onto your brain.
- Use humour. Laughing relaxes people and wins them over. But if anyone has to be the butt of the humour, make it yourself. A sense of humour can turn a good talk into a great one. Read children's joke books to discover the humour they enjoy – it is not generally adult humour!

ILLUSTRATING YOUR TALK

It is important to illustrate your talk, preferably in a way that creates an element of suspense or surprise. This will help you to keep the children's attention, as well as making your talk more memorable. A technique I often use is to start my talk with partly drawn illustrations which I then complete as I go along. 'Ladder lettering' comes into this category.

Ladder lettering has been around for a very long time. It's a great way to create and hold the interest of people of all ages. As far as I know, it was invented in Australia where a shopkeeper used it to advertise his goods. Crowds of people gathered to see if they could guess what the shopkeeper was going to write next, and a passing open-air preacher saw its potential. That is how sketch-board ladder lettering was born. Learning it will take you a little time, patience and persistence, but once you have mastered it you will have a really worthwhile skill.

The best way to start is with a sheet of paper on which you have drawn some squares. With a thick felt pen, practise putting in the marks in order to form the letters. Here I have set out the ladder lettering alphabet for you.

You will see that the marks are always straight and simple, which means that the letters can be revealed rapidly and the words appear as if by magic. Resist the temptation to add any embellishments! Anything other than the alphabet, such as numbers, punctuation, etc., I usually write in the ordinary way.

For a change, I sometimes use ladder lettering on an acetate with an overhead projector. For this I design the layout on my computer and then make a high-resolution colour printout on acetate. You could of course use permanent coloured acetate pens for your initial design. I always put my original acetate into a clear acetate wallet, and then during the talk I draw onto the wallet with washable acetate pens. This makes life much easier when I have two assemblies in the same school, one after the other. All I need to do is take two clear wallets and clean them up when I get home, leaving the original design unscathed for future use. With the development of PowerPoint and Smart Boards it's easier still, and if you have artistic flair and are familiar with the programs, you're well away.

All of the assemblies in this book that use sketch-boards and ladder lettering show the initial layout that you need to prepare in advance and an illustration of the finished sketch-board.

The ultimate labour-saving way to obtain the full-colour artwork necessary to enable OHP or PowerPoint presentation of any illustrated talk in this book is to purchase downloads from the library of files available via **www.childrensministry. co.uk or www.canicholls.com.**

Having said all this, I don't think anything will ever replace the magic of ladder lettering using sketch-board and paints. Children and teachers never seem to tire of it and, being low-tech, it is quite different to what they are used to. It is more labour-intensive, but many a teacher has come up to me after an assembly and said, 'I must learn how to do that!'

Sketch-boards are easily portable and relatively inexpensive. If you are interested in buying one, why not get in touch with Open Air Campaigners via their website: **www.oacgb.org.uk**. They are a very approachable bunch and will point you in the right direction, as there is usually someone in OAC who makes sketch-boards.

If you are going down the sketch-board route, you will also need to find a supplier of inexpensive paper of the right size. The best place to go is your local newspaper. They always have what is known as 'ends of rolls'. When they have finished a print run there is not enough paper left on the rolls to be of any use to them, but it will last you a very long time. And it is possible that they will make no charge if they know it is for children's work. The paper can be neatly and securely held across the sketch-board using large bulldog clips on all four sides.

The other items you will need can be kept in a small toolbox. Store powder paint (red, yellow, blue, green and black) in jars with screw tops, and make sure you have another jar of clear water and five substantial brushes. The toolbox can be purchased from a DIY store, and the powder paints and brushes from a toy shop such as Early Learning Centre.

I have been using ladder lettering for many years and can almost do it with my eyes shut. However, if I am using my sketch-board for an assembly talk I will still pencil in my message first before painting it up. Painting up a word as you're talking and then realising that you have made a mistake is most annoying!

OAC often run courses on sketch-board technique – but here are a few basic tips:

- Practise loading your brush with the right amount of paint, because if you overload your brush, the paint will tend to run down the paper.

- If you paint your lettering boxes over a coloured background, such as yellow, the words will stand out more dramatically than if you were to leave the boxes white.
- Before starting your talk, take the lids off the colours you intend to use and give the paints a stir with their relevant brushes. Then nothing will interrupt your flow.

Whichever medium you use, I would strongly encourage you to persevere with ladder lettering. I guarantee that every time you use it, you will be really pleased with the response.

OBJECT LESSONS

Object lessons are powerful visual metaphors that will guarantee the total attention of every child from 4 to 11 (and all the staff) and at the same time make a point in a way that will be remembered for a long time.

Object lessons can be labour-intensive, often requiring props to be made and a lot of rehearsal in order to look effortless and be successful. But if you are able to make the commitment of time and effort, the rewards will be considerable.

Have you ever thought of taking up conjuring as a hobby? Tricks can be useful when you want to make a point in a particularly memorable way. When you are performing a trick, or object lesson of any kind, and you get to the point that you want to drive home, freeze it into a still picture. It's as if you're posing for a photograph – your audience will 'take' that picture and remember it. (TV commercials often contain still pictures, because it's easier to remember a still image than a moving one.) But poses don't come naturally – they need to be rehearsed.

Some of the assemblies in this book contain object lessons. Choose one of them and have a go. You may surprise yourself. And you'll certainly surprise the children!

WORKING WITH VENT DOLLS (VENTRILOQUISTS' PUPPETS)

It's amazing what you can get away with when using a vent doll. When I first started to use mine, I felt sure that no one was going to 'buy' it. Fifteen years on, I dare not go into a school without it! The children absolutely love it when I walk into an assembly with my puppet, Jimmy. I'm not the world's best ventriloquist, although I'm a lot better now than when I first started. However, I guarantee that if you can pluck up enough courage to give it a go, you will be surprised at what you can do and how the children will respond. With regard to humour, you will of course have to work within your own personality. You will also need to understand what makes children laugh.

Of course, if you do assemblies as a team then you don't have to become a ventriloquist. One of you can operate and be the voice of the puppet from behind a screen.

I will often use a short puppet sketch to lead me into the main assembly talk, but I have also found that I can use a puppet sketch as a talk in itself. This is especially useful if the assembly time is short. In this way the children get to see the puppet and are still given a Christian message. A good way to do this is to tell a Bible story and have the puppet interrupting you and putting a funny twist on the things you are saying.

I have found that with my particular style, the puppet works well with Key Stage 1 and Lower Juniors. Sometimes in a large school there will be separate assemblies for Lower and Upper Juniors. If I am working with the older children only, and my assembly talk includes a short introduction, I may substitute the puppet with an object lesson. At some of my schools, however, I have worked with the puppet for so long that the children wouldn't want anything else. It really is a question of getting to know your schools and their children.

An important thing to remember when using a puppet for the first time, especially with young children, is that it really comes alive to them. Your approach needs to be very gentle. I will often say something along these lines:

'How many of you haven't seen Jimmy before?' *(Wait for some hands to go up.)* 'Well, if Jimmy has not met you before, he might be a little scared. But as long as he knows you're not going to hurt him, he will be OK. You won't hurt Jimmy, will you girls and boys?'

This has the effect of making the children feel protective towards the puppet before they have even seen him. I wait for their response, and when I take him out of the case I go through a routine of him being shy and burying his head in my shoulder. This often gets the children laughing, and after a short while they are used to him. If it's a school that I'm working in for the first time, I will ask one or two teachers to be on the look-out so that they can deal with any child who may be showing signs of concern. It always works a lot better if you can have other people monitoring the situation for you.

The Muppet-type vent dolls you can buy today are great and have soft-looking faces and, I think, are very child friendly. Children are also used to seeing them on television.

After an assembly, I will often get a number of children coming up and asking if they can see Jimmy again. I always resist the temptation to take the puppet out of the case in these situations, and I tell the children that he's asleep now. It then keeps the novelty factor alive, and never fails to produce faces full of excitement when I next go into that school. You will kill the illusion if you just wave the puppet around on demand!

Below are three typical sketches that I use as introductions to lead me into a main assembly talk. Assemblies 21: 'He is Able to Save' and 28: 'Monsters' show how the puppet can also be used in the main assembly talk.

FOLLOW THE RULES

Before getting the puppet out of the case, I tell the children that Jimmy has just started to play football and that he had his first game just the other day. 'Shall we see how he got on?'

YOU	I understand that you had your first game of football the other day?
PUPPET	Yes.
YOU	Did you have a good time?
PUPPET	No.
YOU	Why not?
PUPPET	I got told off.
YOU	Why did you get told off?
PUPPET	I scored a goal.
YOU	You got told off because you scored a goal?

PUPPET	Yes.
YOU	Why did you get told off for scoring a goal?
PUPPET	It was the wrong goal!
YOU	You mean you kicked the ball into your own goal?
PUPPET	Yes.
YOU	Well that was silly. Why did you kick the ball into your own goal? Was it a mistake?
PUPPET	No.
YOU	Well that was really silly. No wonder you got told off. What made you kick the ball into your own goal?
PUPPET	It was the nearest!
YOU	You're supposed to kick the ball into the other team's goal. Why didn't you try to do that?
PUPPET	Too far away and I don't like running.
YOU	But you have got to follow the rules. *(Look at the children.)* He's got to play by the rules, hasn't he children? *(Wait for the children to respond.)*
PUPPET	I don't like the rules, they're silly.
YOU	No, the rules are not silly. The rules are there for a very good purpose.
PUPPET	What's that?
YOU	Well, if you didn't have rules everyone would do their own thing and then you would end up with all sorts of problems. You wouldn't have a proper game at all. It would all be a complete waste of time and it wouldn't be fair to those who wanted to play properly. The Bible teaches that God has rules.
PUPPET	Does God like football?
YOU	I expect God likes to see you play football – when you play it fairly. But I mean that God has rules for us to live by. It's when people don't follow those rules that things start to go wrong – just like it did when you were playing football. Will you try and follow the rules properly next time?
PUPPET	Yes.
YOU	Well, I'm going to tell the boys and girls a story now about someone who didn't follow God's rules. So say 'cheerio' nicely.
PUPPET	Cheerio nicely!
YOU	No, don't say 'cheerio nicely' – say it properly.
PUPPET	It properly!
YOU	No, don't say 'cheerio nicely' and don't say 'it properly'.

PUPPET	Don't say 'cheerio nicely' and don't say 'it properly'?
YOU	No.
PUPPET	All right, if you're sure. Goodbye you smelly rotten lot!
YOU	*(Putting the puppet back into the case)* He didn't mean it.
PUPPET	*(Little voice from the case)* Yes I did!

HONOLULU

I start this sketch by telling the children that Jimmy is talking about going on holiday, so we'll take him out of the case and see where he wants to go.

YOU	You look thoughtful. What are you thinking about?
PUPPET	Holiday.
YOU	Where are you going?
PUPPET	Honolulu.
YOU	I'd like to go there.
PUPPET	You were there yesterday.
YOU	Where?
PUPPET	On the loo-loo!
YOU	Anyway, talking of holidays, do you like flying?
PUPPET	Yes – I saw time fly yesterday.
YOU	How did you see time fly?
PUPPET	I threw my clock out of the window!
YOU	Why did you throw your clock out of the window?
PUPPET	It started ringing.
YOU	Do you mean the alarm went off?
PUPPET	Yes.
YOU	What was the time?
PUPPET	Ten o'clock.
YOU	What, ten o'clock at night?
PUPPET	No, ten o'clock at day.
YOU	You mean ten o'clock in the morning.
PUPPET	Yes.
YOU	Well, you should be up by then.
PUPPET	That's too early.
YOU	What time do you think you should get up?
PUPPET	Three o'clock in the afternoon!
YOU	Three in the afternoon? All the girls and boys are coming out of school by then.

PUPPET	Well, that's a good time to get up then.
YOU	But if you don't go to school, you won't learn anything. And if you don't learn anything, you won't get a good job. And if you don't get a good job, you won't earn any money. And if you don't earn any money, you won't be able to go to places like Honolulu.
PUPPET	I want to go now.
YOU	Where?
PUPPET	On the loo-loo.
YOU	Can you wait until I finish the assembly?
PUPPET	Yes.
YOU	OK. Well, say cheerio.
PUPPET	Cheerio!

(Put the puppet back in the case.)

FEELING SICK

This is a good introduction to the talk about Zacchaeus, Assembly 37: 'Small Man, Big Change. . .'

As I'm getting Jimmy out of the case he says:

PUPPET	I don't feel very well!
YOU	You don't feel very well?
PUPPET	No, I feel sick!
YOU	Why do you feel sick?
PUPPET	Chocolate!
YOU	What do you mean – you've eaten all that chocolate?
PUPPET	Yes. And I feel sick!
YOU	You didn't save any for me?
PUPPET	No. You wasn't there!
YOU	*Weren't* there. . . You could have thought about giving up chocolate for Lent.
PUPPET	What's Lent?

(Explain to puppet what Lent is about – giving up something.)

PUPPET	I'll give up cleaning my teeth! I'll give up washing!
YOU	No, you're supposed to give up something you like, not something you don't like!

PUPPET   What's the point of that?

(Explain the reason for Lent. As an athlete or a footballer needs to train hard to be good at what they do, some people give up things over the 40 days of Lent to train themselves not to be selfish or greedy.)

YOU   Right, well, I've got a story now about someone who gave up something that he really loved. But he didn't just give it up for 40 days – he gave it up for good. Will you listen to the story?

PUPPET   Yes.

YOU   Then say 'cheerio' to the girls and boys.

PUPPET   Cheerio!

(Put the puppet back in the case.)

INTERACTION AND PARTICIPATION

Audience participation always makes for a good assembly. It has the effect of turning passive onlookers into children who are thoroughly engaged with what is taking place. There are four ways in which you can involve the children:

1. **Questions.** Adopt the habit of asking questions as you go through your talk. Include:

    *   Questions that invite children to put their hand up so that you can choose two or three to give you their answer.
    *   Questions requiring a 'yes', 'no' or other one-word answer that the children can call out.
    *   Questions that simply invite the children to think about what you have said, perhaps giving them a few seconds to do so before you continue your talk.

2. **Volunteers.** The talks in this book provide plenty of opportunities for you to invite children to come out to the front and help you. Many (although not all) children love to be in the spotlight, and the other children will enjoy watching their peers perform. Always build up your volunteer and make him or her look good. If you are warm towards your volunteer, it makes all the other children feel warm. But if you make your volunteer feel uncomfortable, all the children will feel the same. Don't bring volunteers out to the front and then make them wait before it's time for them to do their bit. Even just giving them something to hold will make them feel useful.

3. **Drama**. Children love watching drama and taking part in it. If you are a teacher, you will be able to rehearse the children beforehand. Otherwise it's possible to do spontaneous drama to some extent, if you give the children very clear directions. (See Assembly 26: 'Joseph is a Worried Man', which contains an instant nativity play. Not much acting involved, but it works well.)

4. **Songs**. Children love singing, as long as the songs have good strong tunes and they're led with enthusiasm. They particularly enjoy action songs. So always:

   - face the children
   - smile
   - sing loudly (even if you can't sing!)
   - do any actions with exaggeration
   - remember that the children won't put more into their singing than you do

Each assembly in this book has suggested songs and they can all be found in *250 Songs for Children's Praise and Worship* (Kingsway 2006), but sometimes it is better to repeat familiar favourites rather than always teaching new songs. You should check a school's policy on acceptable songs.

PRAYER AND REFLECTION

This is how many people think of prayer: God is at a great distance and can only be contacted by the vicar going through some ritual! But for Christians, God is close, and prayer is simply talking to him like one would talk to another person.

Also, I'm sure God has a sense of humour! And it is possible to build fun into something which is essentially serious. Prayer doesn't have to be sombre.

I often use a '1, 2, 3' routine for the closing prayer. Children love doing it. It ensures that they are all quiet during the prayer, and that they're also quiet afterwards. I have found that it has an element of fun, but then quietens the children back down at the end, which is something you must always be capable of doing. No teacher will thank you for sending the children back to class excited and on a high, leaving them the job of calming everyone down before they can start teaching. The routine goes like this:

When we pray, girls and boys, I like to do my prayer aerobics. I am the fastest in the country, possibly the world, and no one can beat me. Watch this. ONE!

As you call out 'one', quickly put your arms out straight in front of you.

Did you see how quick I am? I always beat everybody! Let's try that again.

Go through that bit of the routine a second time. The children will quickly catch on and will possibly start calling out that they were faster than you, etc.

Now, TWO! . . .

Quickly fold your arms, and again the children will automatically follow your example. They may also call out the number you are saying as they do it, but I then use this opportunity to explain that they have to do it silently, otherwise they lose!

When I say THREE! I put my head down and close my eyes (demonstrate) and then I will say a prayer. If you agree with my prayer you can say 'amen' at the end, because that is what 'amen' means. It simply means that you agree with what is being said.

It is important to explain this before saying a prayer so that you don't run the risk of offending anyone. You are making it obvious that you are giving people a free choice.

When I say FOUR! . . .

Quickly look up with your arms still folded.

I would like to see you all sitting up nice and straight with your arms folded, ready for me to hand back to your teachers. OK, let's do it for real. Are you ready? I'm very quick!

At this point I take up the stance of a cowboy about to challenge someone to a quick-draw shoot-out. Just as the children are anticipating me calling out 'one', I either stamp my foot or cough loudly, putting my hand up to my mouth as I do so. It fools everyone. Even some of the teachers get caught out. Everyone falls about laughing. I then say,

OK, let's be serious now.

I go through the routine again from start to finish but now in serious mode, giving out the signal that this time there is not to be any fooling around. After the prayer and the 'amen' I call out 'four', with my arms folded and looking round at all the children, indicating that the assembly has come to an end and that I want to see them all sitting up nicely with their arms folded and not talking. I will sometimes look around and say,

Let's see who is sitting up the best.

I then look towards the head teacher or teacher in charge of the assembly and say 'thank you', which indicates that I am handing back to them.

You can also use the '1, 2, 3' routine if you are having a time of reflection and you want the children to close their eyes while they're thinking. It is of course important that the children have the opportunity to respond in whatever way is right for them, as long as they treat the prayer time or the reflection time with respect. You can't force anyone to pray!

EMERGENCIES

The motto is: **BE PREPARED!** Always have something up your sleeve.

If you are a teacher, imagine arriving at school to be told that the person taking assembly is off sick, and you have ten minutes to think of something! Or, if you are not a teacher, imagine that a school rings you at the last minute to stand in for someone.

Here are two suggestions which the children will love:

1. Read a brief story from a children's Bible and have a team quiz on it afterwards (divide the entire audience into two – e.g. right & left). Quiz scoring methods could include:

   - Snakes & Ladders (OHP and giant soft dice)
   - Noughts & Crosses (OHP)
   - Basketball (from Early Learning Centre or similar toy shop)
   - Darts (from Early Learning Centre or similar toy shop)

   In each case, the child who gives the correct answer 'has a go'.

   If you look round toy shops such as Early Learning Centre you will come across other ideas for quiz scoring methods. Also, have a look through the Hope Education Catalogue which can be found in most schools.

   End your assembly with a few comments on the point of the story, and a prayer.

2. Pick out a relevant Bible verse and present it as a memory verse. Use the 'Hangman' method on the OHP, but with a pie-chart instead of gallows. This technique is described in detail in Assembly 45: 'Trust or Bust'.

   You could then just say a few words about the verse, and end with a prayer.

   You will need to prepare in advance:

   - A few Bible stories with about ten questions on each of them.
   - Some Bible verses with a few comments on each of them.

Keep these stories, verses and your notes, together with various games and acetates in an Emergency Box or Drawer. Panic will be a thing of the past!

* * *

Note: All suggested songs can be found in *250 Songs for Children's Praise and Worship* (Kingsway 2006) – song numbers in brackets.

A BIT OF A MESS

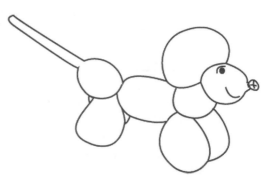

VALUES: Choosing right; Friendship

BIBLE REFERENCE: Psalm 119:9

TEACHING POINT: The Bible teaches us that God's way is the best way.

NOTES: I personalise this talk by using some of my own testimony. The part of my testimony that I use is quite general and may be relevant to you. If it doesn't match your experience, you may wish to change the narrative. Alternatively, you could relate it as the experience of someone you know. Instructions are provided for the use of a sketch-board – the ladder letter words are underlined.

YOU WILL NEED: Five modelling balloons (already inflated); balloon pump and spare balloons (in case any of those being used should burst); prepared sketch-board and paints, PowerPoint or OHP acetate and pens (see introductory section on ladder lettering or visit **www.canicholls.com** and **www.childrensministry.co.uk** for information on how to purchase downloads).

I wonder if you ever feel like this? <u>A BIT OF A MESS</u>.

Sometimes our lives can feel as though nothing seems to be going right. I have found that it is a good idea to surround myself with lots of friends. Then, when I need help, there's always someone to turn to – and, of course, they can turn to me too. But there can sometimes be a problem with friends and you can end up in a bit of a <u>MUDDLE</u>.

Draw in the first sad face.

Put your hand up if you've ever felt that someone has let you down or made you sad. *(Pause.)* Now, put your hand up if *you* have ever let anyone down or made someone sad. *(Pause.)*

No matter how hard we try, we all make mistakes because we are all human. Sometimes we fall out over something and have an argument. Sometimes we can be given the wrong information, or we get confused by what we're told and don't ask for a better explanation. The other day I asked a person for directions and I ended up getting completely lost – but that was because I didn't listen properly!

The Bible teaches, and Christians believe, that God has given us directions for living a good life: the Bible. The trouble is, we don't always like being told what to do. Do you always listen to your teachers and do what they ask? No, sometimes we can be naughty.

I can remember there were times when I was naughty at school because I wanted my own way. I suffered with 'I disease'. Do you know what 'I disease' is? It's 'I want this, I want that, I want my own way and I want it now!' When we don't go the way God wants us to go, the Bible calls it <u>SIN</u>. Notice how the middle letter of the word 'sin' is 'I'. Sin is a terrible thing and it can cause our lives to get really <u>MIXED UP</u>.

Draw in the second sad face.

There was a time when my life was all mixed up like that. I wasn't always sure what I should do. But that was before I met a very special friend who has never let me down. I wonder if you can guess who that friend is? I will give you a clue.

Draw in the third sad face and the cross – draw the downward stroke over the letter 'I' of the word SIN, and the cross stroke through the 'S' and the 'N'. Give the children the opportunity to guess the name of your friend.

The Bible teaches that Jesus came to cross out our sin by dying for us on a cross so that we can be friends with God. Now, when I became friends with God, and started to find out how he wanted me to live my life, something strange happened. I stopped feeling all mixed up, and my life didn't seem to be in a muddle anymore. Let me show you what I mean.

Today we are going to have a competition! Who would like to have a go?

Pick four volunteers, preferably older children.

I'm going to make something, and I want you to watch what I do very carefully.

Model a balloon dog or similar. Then give each volunteer an inflated balloon.

Now, when I say 'Go!' I want you all to start making a balloon animal. You can copy what I did or make one of your own. 'Ready, steady, go!'

This can be very funny because you will end up with weird shapes and sizes, which is exactly what you want. Encourage the children to twist and turn the balloons however they choose. You can play some fast music while this is going on. Allow about 30 seconds and when the time is up, ask the other children to give your helpers a big round of applause as you hold up their efforts. Then ask them to sit down.

Now children, I want to explain something. I was able to make a good balloon animal because I have made lots of them and I know what I am doing. My helpers are not experts and so they ended up in a bit of a mess, not really knowing what to do for the best.

The Bible teaches that God is an expert in sorting out our lives (*draw in the smiley face*) and that is why he has given us rules to live by so that we don't have to end up in a muddle. I can choose not to bother with God's rules, but experience has taught me that it is always better to learn from someone who really knows what they are doing.

SUGGESTED SONGS:
I can do all things (97)
Jubilate, everybody (135)
Lord, tell me your ways (145)

SUGGESTED PRAYER:
Forgive us, Father, when we get in a bit of a mess by going our own way, saying things we shouldn't say and doing things we shouldn't do. Thank you for the Bible which teaches us your way – the best way. Amen.

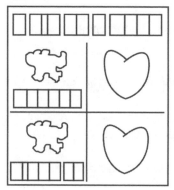

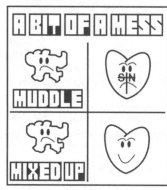

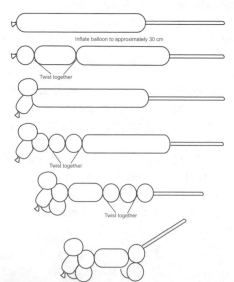

Instructions for making a balloon animal

Inflate balloon to approximately 30 cm

Twist together

Twist together

Twist together

pdf available

A CHRISTMAS GIFT

VALUE: Gratefulness

BIBLE REFERENCES: John 3:16; Ephesians 1:4–5

TEACHING POINT: God sent the wonderful gift of Jesus.

YOU WILL NEED: A small present (something a child could use in school such as a pen, pencil or plastic ruler) wrapped in Christmas paper; prepared illustrations on OHP acetates or PowerPoint (visit **www.canicholls.com** and **www.childrensministry.co.uk** for information on how to purchase downloads).

Show the picture of a Christmas present.

Who likes receiving Christmas presents? What are the best presents?

Let two or three children tell you what their best present would be.

I love being given a present – it's so exciting when you start to unwrap it and try and guess what is inside. But I have also found, as I've got older, that I enjoy giving presents too – especially if you know it is a present that someone really wants. Now, at the moment you might not be in a position to buy presents for people because they cost too much money. But one day you'll be able to. And then, how will you go about it? Let me see if I can help you.

Show the picture of a man in prison.

Here is a person who has been very naughty. In fact, he has been so naughty that he has been sent to prison. He has a family at home who are feeling sad because he is not going to be with them at Christmas.

Now tell me, what would be the best Christmas present you could give this man and his family – what would make them all really happy?

Ask the children to put up their hands and choose one to answer – they will normally give the answer you want.

Yes, freedom. It might be nice to give him a book or some pens and paper, but the thing that he really needs in order to be happy is his freedom. So if you are going to give a person a gift with the idea of making them happy, it should be something they need. In order to do that, we have to. . .

Show the picture of a person with the thought bubble and the word 'Plan'.

. . .plan our gift. We need to spend some time thinking about what it is we are going to give.

The Bible teaches that God has given us a gift – a gift that we all need and that will make us very happy – and that God *planned* that gift long before he gave it to us. It says in the Bible, 'Because of his love, God had already decided that through Jesus Christ he would make us his children.'

Once I have planned my gift, once I have decided what it is I would like to give, I then have to ask myself this question. Am I prepared. . .

Show the picture of a person with the thought bubble with a £ sign.

. . .to pay the price? When you give a person a gift, there is a cost. Not only will it cost you money, but it will also cost you time and effort. You spend time thinking about what it is you are going to get, then you go round the shops until you find what you're looking for, and then you hand over your money. And when you get home, you have to spend some more time. . .

Show the picture of a man wrapping a gift.

. . .preparing it in a way that makes it acceptable to the person you are giving it to. You need to wrap your present.

Show the picture of the cross.

When God sent his gift – Jesus – he didn't wrap him in colourful paper. He wrapped him in the form of a human being. God knew that he would need to send Jesus in a way that would be acceptable to the world.

We can read in the Bible how Jesus grew up teaching people about God and how much he loves us. He explained how our sin separates us from God and that he had come into this world to make things right, so that we can live with him for ever in heaven. In order to do that, he had to take the punishment for all the naughty things we think and say and do, by dying on the cross.

Take out of your bag your small gift wrapped in Christmas paper.

Now, I would like to give someone a gift before I go. Who really wants a gift? I only have one. Who is sitting up the straightest?

Pick the child who looks keener than anyone else.

You seem really keen, so I think I'd like to give it to you. But what do you say?

Ask the child his/her name and get him/her to say 'please' and 'thank you'. This is important because you want to press home the point about asking God and saying 'thank you', etc.

I only had one small gift and sadly not enough for everyone, but I did want to give my gift to someone who really wanted it. In order for [*name*] to get that gift, he/she had to receive it from me.

The Bible teaches, and Christians believe, that Jesus is a gift that we not only need, but that we also really have to want. Of course, God's love is far bigger than the gift I've just given away. In fact, his love is so big that there *is* enough for everyone. All we have to do is say 'sorry' for all the bad things we have done and ask for his forgiveness – not forgetting, of course, to say 'please' and 'thank you'. God is always willing to forgive us, and he is always willing to give to us. But there is one really important thing we need to do: we do have to *receive* his gift.

I wonder, what will *you* decide to do with God's gift?

SUGGESTED SONGS:
Child in a manger born (22)
Come and join the celebration (25)

SUGGESTED PRAYER:
Dear Father in heaven, thank you that you loved me so much that you were prepared to send your Son into this world in order that I can be made right with you. Thank you for the wonderful gift of Jesus. Amen.

A FRESH START

VALUES: Forgiveness; Trust

BIBLE REFERENCE: Genesis 6:5 – 9:17

TEACHING POINT: God can help us make a fresh start.

NOTES: This talk is ideal for the start of a new school year, although with a slight change of words at the beginning it could be used at any time. Instructions are provided for the use of a sketch-board – the ladder letter words are underlined.

YOU WILL NEED: Prepared sketch-board and paints, PowerPoint or OHP acetate and pens (see introductory section on ladder lettering or visit **www.canicholls.com** and **www.childrensministry.co.uk** for information on how to purchase downloads).

Everyone in this school has recently made one of these: <u>A FRESH START</u> – because it is a new school year. Many of you have gone up a year. Some of you have just started at this school. It probably feels strange – but it's exciting too, isn't it?

The Bible tells us that thousands of years ago, God made a fresh start. Almost all the people who lived on the earth at that time were very bad indeed. . .

Draw fighting stick-men.

. . .selfish, violent, always fighting and quarrelling. And they couldn't care less about God. This filled God's heart with <u>PAIN</u>.

At school, if you want to be friends with someone but they don't want to be friends with you, it hurts, doesn't it?

Well, the Bible tells us that God was hurt because these people didn't want to know him. All except for a man called Noah and his family. They loved God and they had managed to stay good in spite of being surrounded by very bad people. It's not easy, is it, to do the right thing when other people are doing the wrong thing and make fun of you and say you're a goody-goody? Does that happen at school sometimes? Sometimes it takes real courage to be good.

God told Noah, 'I'm sorry I created these people. I'm going to destroy them by flooding the whole earth with water, and start all over again. But I'm going to save you, Noah, and your family, so I want you to make an ark.'

Do you know what an ark is?

Explain what the ark was as you draw it.

Noah had to make an ark out of wood, 140 metres long (that's as long as one-and-a-half football pitches), and as high as a very tall house, with a roof and lots of different rooms inside.

It sounds crazy, doesn't it? Not a cloud in the sky or a puddle on the ground, and God tells Noah to build an enormous boat! Of course, Noah couldn't go to the DIY shop for the wood – he had to chop down hundreds of trees. And he didn't have a chain-saw either! Everyone thought Noah was completely potty!

When the ark was finished, God said to Noah, 'Now go inside with your family, and take with you a male and female of every kind of bird, animal and reptile. And take a *lot* of food!'

Sure enough, when they were all safely inside the ark and had shut the door. . .

Add rain to your picture.

. . .the rain started. Not just pitter-patter rain. It *fell* down, non-stop, for over a month. The water level got higher and higher until it covered the bushes; it covered the trees; it covered the hills; and it even covered the mountains!

Draw the different water levels as you are speaking.

The ark floated on top of the water. The flood lasted for five whole months, and every person and every creature that wasn't safely inside the ark was drowned.

It can't have been easy inside the ark. Imagine . . . all those animals! What would have been the worst thing, do you think? There must have been an awful PONG! Sometimes being a Christian and doing what God wants isn't easy!

But then the flood waters began to go down and the ark came to rest – thump – on a mountain. I expect Noah thought, 'Thank goodness for that!'

Noah sent out this creature.

Draw dove.

Do you know what kind of bird it is? *(Allow the children to answer.)*

When the dove came flying back. . .

Draw leaf.

. . .with an olive leaf in its beak, Noah knew the water must have gone right down and it was safe to leave. And so they all staggered out of the ark. They looked around and listened, and they noticed something about this new world: PEACE. There was no more fighting, no more quarrelling, and they could make a completely fresh start.

Today we don't have to build an ark if we want our lives to have a fresh start. The Bible teaches that 2,000 years ago, Jesus came down from heaven and died on a cross to take the punishment for all our selfishness. Christians believe that all we need to do is to stop going our own way and accept God's forgiveness, and then we can begin a brand-new friendship with Jesus that will last for ever. His peace will be in our hearts.

God was pleased with Noah because he'd trusted him. And so God made this

<u>PROMISE</u>. He said, 'Never again will I cover the earth with a flood. And this will be a reminder of my promise.'

Draw rainbow.

What is it? Whenever I see a rainbow in the sky, it reminds me of God's promise in the Bible – that he wants to save us and not to harm us. But also that he doesn't want us to hurt him by going our own way.

But if we do make a mistake and get it wrong, the Bible tells us that, with God, we can always make a fresh start.

SUGGESTED SONGS:
Father, I place into your hands (44)
Rise and shine (64)

SUGGESTED PRAYER:
Dear Father, forgive me when I hurt others by the things I say and do. Help me not to give up when things get difficult, and to remember that I can always look to you for the answers. Thank you that we can always make a fresh start. Amen.

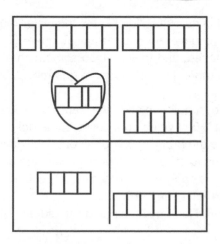

BE COOL!

VALUES: Courage; Facing peer pressure

BIBLE REFERENCE: Daniel 3

TEACHING POINT: God will always help us to resist pressure to do the wrong thing.

YOU WILL NEED: Prepared illustrations on OHP acetates or PowerPoint (visit **www.canicholls.com** and **www.childrensministry.co.uk** for information on how to purchase downloads); two additional acetates or slides with the words: 'When Life Gets Hot' and 'Be Cool!'

This is a story from the Bible about three very cool young men. . .

Show picture of three young men.

. . .Shadrach, Meshach and Abednego. They lived hundreds of years before Jesus was born. They had been captured from their home in Jerusalem, and taken off to another country by a foreign king with a long name – Nebuchadnezzar. Shadrach, Meshach and Abednego were bright young men, and so the king had given them important jobs in his kingdom.

But this king – Nebuchadnezzar – was conceited and very rich. He liked to throw his weight around and make everyone do what he wanted. He decided. . .

Show picture of statue.

. . .to have a huge gold statue of himself built. It was 3 metres wide and 30 metres tall – two or three times as high as this room.

The king told all the important people in the land to come and see his statue. Then he ordered them, 'When the music starts up, you must fall down and worship my statue.' Wasn't that ridiculous? Would you have done it, if you'd been there? It would have been a bit like bowing down to this overhead projector.

Demonstrate! I act it out by bowing down to the OHP and talking to it, telling it all about my problems. This enables the children to see how ridiculous it is to worship objects, but does it in a humorous way.

But – there was a catch. The king said, 'If anyone doesn't bow down and worship my statue, they will be thrown into a fiery furnace!' Well, of course no one wanted to be thrown into a great big fire. They were scared. So, as soon as the music started up. . .

Show picture of crowd surrounding statue.

. . .everyone bowed down and worshipped the statue. And they all looked pretty stupid!

Everyone, that is, except – you've guessed it – Shadrach, Meshach and Abednego. They loved God, and they knew it was wrong to worship anything or anyone other than God. So they stayed standing up. The king. . .

Show picture of angry king.

. . .was furious. He said, 'I'll give you one more chance. If you don't bow down and worship my statue right now, I'll have you thrown into the fire, and then you'll be sorry!'

But the three young men said to the king, 'God is able to save us from the flames. But, *even if he doesn't,* we will not worship your statue!' Sometimes, boys and girls, other people might want you to join in something that you know is wrong – like cheating or stealing or telling lies, or perhaps bullying, or even taking drugs. It takes courage to say 'no', especially when other people around you are doing these things.

Well, Shadrach, Meshach and Abednego had the courage, even though they were probably shaking inside.

The king was beside himself with rage. 'Make the furnace seven times hotter!' he screamed. . .

Show picture of fire.

. . .and then he told his strongest soldiers to tie up Shadrach, Meshach and Abednego and throw them into the fire. So that's what they did. But the fire was so fierce by this time that, as they pushed the men in, the flames leapt out and killed the soldiers!

Then the king gasped with amazement. . .

Show picture of four men in fire.

. . .because he saw the young men walking about in the furnace, untied and as calm as if they were walking down the street. He could hardly believe what he saw. He said, 'Didn't we throw three men into the furnace? But I can see four men in there now! And the fourth one looks like a son of God!'

I think that fourth person was Jesus. The Bible teaches that Jesus has always existed – that he was alive long before he was born into this world as a baby at the first Christmas. The Bible teaches that Jesus came to live on this earth 2,000 years ago, and that he died on a cross so that God can forgive us for our sins, if we come to him and say 'sorry', and give our lives to him. The Bible teaches that Jesus rose from the dead and that he is alive today.

King Nebuchadnezzar didn't know about Jesus, of course, but he realised he was seeing the power of the living God at work, protecting the three young men from the flames. That made his statue look pretty pathetic!

The king called out, 'Shadrach, Meshach and Abednego, come out, come here!'

Show picture of the three young men.

They came out, and not a single hair of their heads was singed. Their clothes weren't scorched. And they didn't even smell of smoke. They really were cool!

At last the king understood why the young men had been willing to die rather than worship a statue. He really respected them for that, and he promoted them to more important jobs in his kingdom.

Sometimes it's difficult to do what's right when that means going against the crowd.

Show words: WHEN LIFE GETS HOT

It can be frightening if people threaten you if you don't do what they want, and lonely if they call you names or don't want to be friends with you anymore. It's hard to say 'no' when you're shaking inside.

Now and then we all go through what seems like a fiery furnace – not a real fire, but very difficult situations. But, as a Christian, I know that whatever I have to go through, I don't have to go through it alone. Jesus always helps me. I believe he's there, even though I can't see him. And I'm quite sure that he's far more powerful than anything or anyone else.

Show words: BE COOL!

He helps me to be cool! Remember – it's cool to have the courage to say 'no'.

SUGGESTED SONGS:
Be bold, be strong (11)
My God is so big (157)
We must be strong (226)

SUGGESTED PRAYER:
Dear Father, please give me the courage to stand up for what is right.
Thank you that with you we are never alone and need never be afraid.
Amen.

BUBBLE, BUBBLE, TOIL AND TROUBLE!

VALUE: Trust

BIBLE REFERENCES: Matthew 11:28; John 16:33

TEACHING POINT: Trust Jesus to help us with our problems.

NOTES: This is a short object lesson that may be useful if you have limited time, or if you have extra time to fill at the end of an assembly on a similar theme. You will need to purchase some thin plywood and some bubble-wrap that has large bubbles. (The smaller bubbles will work fine, but the larger ones will work better from a visual point of view, and create a louder pop!)

YOU WILL NEED: A piece of bubble-wrap, approximately 1 m square, a piece of thin plywood, approximately 1 m square, with the word JESUS clearly written on it.

Imagine you're a bubble! Now think of a word that rhymes with 'bubbles'.

Ask for suggestions until you get the answer, 'troubles'.

It's very easy to pop bubbles and destroy them.

Demonstrate with your piece of bubble-wrap.

And this is what our troubles can do to us.

Continue popping bubbles at the edge as you say. . .

- School can be very hard work *(pop!)*
- People can be unkind to you *(pop!)*
- Maybe you're feeling lonely *(pop!)*

Do you think that when someone becomes a Christian, all their troubles go away? No, of course they don't. Jesus actually said, 'In this world you will have trouble.' But there is a big difference when someone is a Christian – because *Jesus* doesn't go away either.

Place the bubble-wrap on the floor. Show the children the plywood board with the word JESUS on it, and then place it on top of the bubble-wrap. Invite two of the children to stand on the board, or stand on it yourself. The bubbles will remain intact.

How do you think the bubbles are feeling? *(Under pressure!)*
But can you hear them popping? *(No!)*
When we're worried or upset or afraid, Christians believe that Jesus knows all about our troubles, and he feels our feelings. He will help us through our troubles and safely out the other side.
When we have troubles. . .

Hold up the board with the word JESUS on it.

. . .the Bible teaches that all we have to do is trust Jesus, and not give up. Then. . .

Hold up the sheet of bubble wrap.

. . .we'll be just like these bubbles which have amazingly survived such a great weight!

SUGGESTED SONGS
Don't worry (37)
I once was frightened of spiders (100)

SUGGESTED PRAYER:
Dear heavenly Father, thank you that you are always there for me in times of trouble. Help me this day to face all my problems, and please guide my thoughts, my words and my actions. Amen.

CARING, SHARING HANNAH

VALUES: Caring; Sharing

BIBLE REFERENCES: 1 Samuel 1:1–24, 2:18–19; John 3:16

TEACHING POINT: God is gracious, and we should aim to be gracious too.

NOTES: Instructions are provided for the use of a sketch-board – the ladder letter words are underlined.

YOU WILL NEED: Prepared sketch-board and paints, PowerPoint or OHP acetate and pens (see introductory section on ladder lettering or visit **www.canicholls.com** and **www.childrensministry.co.uk** for information on how to purchase downloads).

I would like to start today by asking if you know what this word means? <u>RARE</u>

Allow some of the children to answer your question.

Did you know that each one of you is a rare person because you are unique? There is only one of you. No two people are the same. There is no one in the world exactly like you, there never has been, and there never will be again. And that makes you very special. There are rare *qualities* that we can only see in some people. Maybe you have some of these qualities – such as being kind and caring. If you have, then I guarantee that you will always be following the school rules.

Often you will see school rules written up on assembly hall walls, and can draw the children's attention to them.

The person in my story today was a rare person, and I want us to look at some of the reasons why. It wasn't because she had beautiful hair. . .

Draw in the plaits.

. . .or because she had beautiful eyes. . .

Paint in the eyes.

. . .or nose. . .

Draw in the nose.

. . .or mouth.

Draw in the mouth. Aim to make the face look quite ridiculous, as it never fails to make the children laugh.

Can anyone tell me what a palindrome is?

If none of the children can answer your question, explain that it is a word that reads the same backwards as forwards.

Well, this young lady had a name that was a palindrome. Her name was

HANNAH. Now, I was looking up names in a book, and found that the meaning of the name Hannah is <u>GRACE</u>. This is a quality that we don't always see in people. Can anyone tell me what the word 'grace' means?

Allow some of the children to answer, and then explain in your own words about grace being undeserved favour.

The Bible teaches that God is always gracious – full of grace – and willing to forgive people if they ask him to. How do you react when a person does something that upsets you? Are you gracious and willing to forgive them? Or do you find that difficult to do?

Anyway, Hannah was a sad lady because she didn't have any children of her own, and in those days a woman could be looked down upon if she didn't have children. There was one particular person who made fun of Hannah and called her names. This made Hannah feel really bad. So what do you think she did? This was another rare quality that Hannah had. She didn't try and get her own back like a lot of people would, but she turned to <u>PRAYER</u>.

Draw in face of person praying.

Something else we can learn from the Bible is that life's battles are not always best fought using our own strength, but with God's help – and that with God, nothing is impossible.

So, Hannah took her troubles to God in prayer. She made a promise to God. She promised that if God allowed her to have a son, she would give him back to God by allowing him to serve God in the temple. Well, God answered Hannah's prayer, and eventually she gave birth to a baby boy whom she named Samuel. Hannah kept her promise, and when Samuel was old enough she took him to live in the temple so that he would grow up learning how to serve God by helping the priest.

Even though Samuel lived in the temple and grew up there, Hannah never forgot about him. Every year she would go and visit him and take a little robe that she'd made for him to wear in the temple.

Draw in coat.

This was a bit like having a school uniform. You see, this was another of Hannah's qualities. She would always <u>CARE</u>. She cared for Samuel. Hannah was a caring person – she had a caring heart.

Are you a person who cares for others? Or are you a person who only cares for yourself?

Can you imagine how difficult it must have been for Hannah to give up her son Samuel to live at the temple? I would like you to think of someone you really love. Now imagine what it would be like to give up that person and send them away to be with someone else so that someone else can benefit.

As well as giving us the story of Hannah, the Bible teaches us about God, and how God gave up his Son, Jesus, so that we can benefit. Hannah had a godly nature because she was willing to <u>SHARE</u>. She was willing to share her son, Samuel, with God. Are you a person who is willing to share with others?

All these qualities we have been talking about, we can also see in Jesus.

Draw in the cross.

But when we do the opposite of what we have been talking about – when we are unkind and selfish – we create a massive division between ourselves and God who just wants to love us. The Bible teaches that Jesus is the only one who can bridge that gap. He is the only one because he has never sinned – never done anything wrong. Not only that, Jesus is always gracious, always forgiving. When people were cruel to him, he didn't want to get his own back. And he always cared for others. And, more than anything else, he was willing to share heaven with everyone who turned to him – and the Bible tells us he still is.

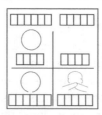

SUGGESTED SONGS:
Father, I place into your hands (44)
Think of a world without any flowers (212)

SUGGESTED PRAYER:
Dear heavenly Father, I am grateful that you were willing to share your Son, Jesus, so that I may benefit. Help me, too, to have a caring and sharing nature. Amen.

CASUALTY!

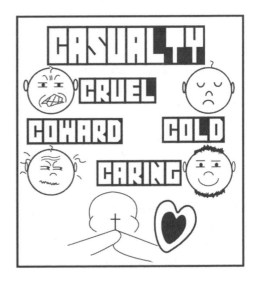

VALUES: Caring; Love; Respect

BIBLE REFERENCE: Luke 10:25–37

TEACHING POINT: Help me respond to the needs of others in the way that God wants me to.

NOTES: Instructions are provided for the use of a sketch-board – the ladder letter words are underlined.

YOU WILL NEED: Prepared sketch-board and paints, PowerPoint or OHP acetate and pens (see introductory section on ladder lettering or visit **www.canicholls.com** and **www.childrensministry.co.uk** for information on how to purchase downloads).

This is one of the stories Jesus told, and I've called it: <u>CASUALTY!</u>

Once upon a time there was a man who set out on a long walk from Jerusalem to a town called Jericho. Half way there, he was set on by muggers.

Draw in vicious face.

They beat him up, and took all his money and most of his clothes. And then they left him lying in the road, groaning. Not a pretty sight! That wasn't very nice, was it? The muggers were <u>CRUEL</u>.

After a while, a priest came along. This looked hopeful. After all, priests were important men who were always telling people to do the right thing.

Draw in snooty face.

But this priest seemed to be in an awful hurry. He didn't stop. He didn't even slow down! He was probably thinking, 'I haven't got time to get involved. I've got far more important things to do. There's bound to be someone else along in a minute.' He just passed by on the other side of the road. Do you think he should have stopped, boys and girls? Yes, he ought to have stopped and helped the wounded man, but his heart was <u>COLD</u>.

A short time later, a worker from the temple came along in a nice, clean white robe. Things looked hopeful again, but he didn't stop either. He was probably thinking, 'Yuk! What a mess! I don't want to get my nice, clean robe all dirty! Anyway, this bloke looks a bit rough – probably brought it all on himself – been drinking and got into a fight. And, who knows – if I stop and help him, the people who attacked him might come back and attack me. Too risky!'

Draw in scared face.

So, he too passed by on the other side. He was a <u>COWARD</u>. And the wounded man lay there thinking, 'Nobody cares about me!'

But wait a minute. . .

(You can make hoof sound effects with empty coconut shells at this point if you wish.)

. . .who's this I hear coming along on a donkey?

This man looked strange. He was a foreigner from Samaria – a Samaritan. People didn't like the Samaritans much, because they looked a bit different.

Draw in swarthy face.

It's the same today, unfortunately. Some people dislike anyone who's a bit different from them, or who comes from another country. That's called prejudice, and it's a horrible thing – and a very unfair thing too, as we'll find out in a minute.

So, people looked down their noses at the Samaritans and usually tried to avoid them. This didn't look at all hopeful for our injured friend.

But, the Samaritan stopped! 'Goodness gracious!' he said. 'What on earth has happened to you?' The wounded man could only groan. The Samaritan got down from his donkey, got out his first aid kit and patched the man up with ointment and bandages. Then he gently lifted him up onto his donkey, and off they went into the sunset – to an inn. *(Clip-clop effects.)*

The Samaritan booked the wounded man into a room, put him to bed and sat up with him all night to make sure he was OK. In the morning, the man was feeling quite a bit better. The Samaritan gave the innkeeper some money and said, 'Please keep my friend here until he's really better. I've got to go to work now, but if there's any more to pay, I'll give you the money when I come back.' The Samaritan was <u>CARING</u>.

Wasn't he kind to do all that? Why do you think he did it – why did he give up his time, his money and his sleep?

Let the children make some suggestions, and then draw a small heart and ask:

What did he have in his heart?

The children will realise that the answer is 'love'.

Yes, he did it because he felt love for the victim. Why do you think Jesus told this story?

Let the children make some suggestions and acknowledge all their ideas.

Jesus wanted to teach us that it's right to help someone in distress, even if no one else bothers, and even if we don't know them, and even if it's rather inconvenient. Jesus wants us to love the people around us and be kind to them – whatever they look like and whatever nationality they happen to be.

But what about the times when *you* are hurt or upset – at school or at home – and it all seems so unfair and as if no one else cares? At times like that, the Bible tells us that Jesus is there with you, just like the Good Samaritan. He wants to take care of you – if you'll let him – because he loves you. You are very, very precious to him – so precious that 2,000 years ago, the Bible tells us. . .

Draw a cross.

. . .he died on a cross to take the punishment for all the things we've ever done wrong, so that God can forgive us and we can live with him for ever.

Christians believe that if you ask him to, Jesus will fill up *your* heart with *his* love – not so you can keep it all to yourself, but so that you can keep on and on and on sharing it with other people. And the interesting thing about love is, the more we share it. . .

Draw a big heart around the small heart. . .

the bigger it grows.

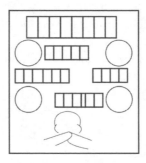

COUNTING THE COST

VALUES: Courage; Facing peer pressure; Generosity

BIBLE REFERENCE: Mark 2:13–17

TEACHING POINT: The cost of choosing to follow Jesus.

NOTES: Instructions are provided for the use of a sketch-board – the ladder letter words are underlined.

YOU WILL NEED: Prepared sketch-board and paints, PowerPoint or OHP acetate and pens (see introductory section on ladder lettering or visit **www.canicholls.com** and **www.childrensministry.co.uk** for information on how to purchase downloads).

Start by asking the children if they have a favourite hobby, and allow a few of them to respond.

Some people like football, some people like collecting things. Personally I like [*name your hobby*].

Now, the name of the person in my story today is Levi, and Levi had a favourite hobby. I bet you won't guess what it was! Can you see what it was? <u>COUNTING</u>.

Yes, the favourite hobby of Levi was counting. But not counting any old thing. No, Levi loved counting money! In fact, he loved counting money so much that when he left school, he got a job as a tax collector. Can anyone tell me what tax collectors did?

Allow some of the children to respond.

These were people who worked for the authorities, and they went round collecting money from everyone else. We still have to pay taxes today, of course, but in those days, tax collectors were not very well liked because they would often cheat people. They did this by collecting more money than they should have done, and then they would put the extra money into their own pockets.

One day, when Jesus was visiting the town where Levi lived, he saw Levi sitting at his table counting his money. Little did Levi know that something was about to happen that would completely change his life for ever. As Jesus walked past, he <u>CALLED</u> Levi.

Jesus said, 'Follow me!' And do you know what Levi did? He left all his money, there and then, and he got up and followed Jesus. There was something about Jesus. Levi knew that when Jesus looked at him, nothing was hidden. Just by looking at him, Jesus could see all Levi's lies and deceit. But, at the same time, Jesus somehow made him feel special. But why did Jesus call Levi to follow him?

The Bible teaches that God knows all about us. He knows about all the good things we do and about all the bad things too. And even if we have been really bad, he never stops loving us. To God we are so precious.

Draw diamond.

Just imagine, if you had a very expensive diamond you wouldn't want to lose it, would you? You would want to look after it and keep it in a safe place. You wouldn't let it out of your sight. Can anybody tell me where diamonds come from, or where they are found?

Allow some of the children to respond.

If you found a diamond deep under the ground, you probably wouldn't realise how precious it was because it would be all dirty and shapeless, just like any other rock. It takes a lot of work to reveal the beauty that is really there. When they are first found, diamonds are not as we see them in a jeweller's window, all sparkly and shiny. But the people who trade in diamonds know that when they are cut in a certain way and highly polished, the true beauty of the diamond can be revealed and they then become very desirable and people will pay a lot of money for them.

The Bible teaches that God looks at us in the same way. He can see that when all the bad things are removed – like bad thoughts, bad words and bad deeds – we become like precious shiny diamonds. Jesus could see that deep down Levi was a good person, and that he just needed working on.

Even though Levi had not been an honest man, Jesus had called him. And Levi felt special because he had been CHOSEN. Jesus still calls people to follow him today. I wonder what you will decide to do if you sense in your heart that Jesus is calling you. One thing you have to know is that following Jesus is not easy, and it will COST. Let's see how much it might cost us.

Jesus had made Levi feel very special, and so Levi wanted to show his thanks. He did this by throwing a big party. It was fantastic.

Draw in the food.

There was chicken, apple pie, jelly and ice cream – all the most delicious things you could want to eat. People could hardly believe their eyes! Levi was giving food away for free! You see, as soon as Levi had started to follow Jesus, he had CHANGED.

Levi had become a changed man. At one time, if people had asked Levi for anything, he would have told them to go away. But now he had become generous and he wanted to give things to people. Following Jesus also meant that he had to stop using bad words and stop doing naughty things. We have to be the same if we are going to follow Jesus. And, if we are going to be generous, it can cost us both time and money.

Draw in THE.

But, while Levi was having his party with all his new-found friends, there were some other people around who thought they knew best. They were the religious leaders of the day – called the Pharisees. When they saw Jesus mixing with the people who they called 'sinners', they thought that Jesus had lost the plot. Not only that, they also thought that anyone who followed Jesus had lost the plot!

It is still the same today. Sometimes, following Jesus can cost you your friends or your reputation. There will be people who think they know better than you and believe that you have lost the plot. If you are going to follow Jesus, you do need to count the cost. But I have found that with a friend like Jesus, neither counting the cost nor paying the cost is ever a problem, because he is always there to help me.

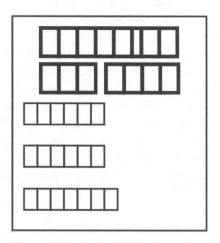

SUGGESTED SONGS:
Be bold, be strong (11)
One in a million (168)

SUGGESTED PRAYER:
Dear Father, please help me in difficult times when people make fun of me. Help me not to worry about what other people think. Help me to see things your way and to always be truthful and honest, whatever the cost. Amen.

DARING DANIEL

VALUES: Love; Trust

BIBLE REFERENCE: Daniel 6:1–28

TEACHING POINT: You can trust God.

NOTES: If you wish, the end of this assembly is the perfect place to add a gospel message about God wanting us to put our trust in Jesus. There is also a parallel that can be drawn between Jesus going to the cross and Daniel going to the lions. Both entrusted their lives into God's hands, etc.

YOU WILL NEED: Prepared illustrations on OHP acetates or PowerPoint (visit **www.canicholls.com** and **www.childrensministry.co.uk** for information on how to purchase downloads); Mr Men books (you will need to prepare additional illustrations of Mr Clever, Mr Mean, Mr Worry and Mr Happy on the sketch-board, OHP acetates or PowerPoint); a small piece of carved wood or chess piece.

Today I want to tell you the story of a man called Daniel. Daniel lived in a far-off place called Babylon, 600 years before Jesus was born. Babylon was in the land that today is called Iraq.

Show the picture of Mr Clever.

Do you know which Mr Man this is? You can see he's wearing glasses – that's a big clue!

Allow two or three children to give you an answer.

Yes, that's right, it's Mr Clever. We all know that people who wear glasses are clever, don't we?

If you wear glasses, you can say this tongue-in-cheek whilst drawing attention to the fact that you are also wearing glasses, by 'adjusting' them!

Daniel was a clever man. But not only was Daniel clever, he was also a man who could be trusted. Now, if you are a person who can be trusted, your teacher may ask you to help by doing certain jobs. It was no different for Daniel, but it wasn't the schoolteacher who asked for Daniel's help, it was the king – King Darius.

Show the picture of Daniel with King Darius.

King Darius said to Daniel, 'Oh Daniel, it's so difficult trying to run this country all on my own. I need someone I can trust to help me. I wondered if you would be interested?' 'Thank you,' said Daniel. 'I will do my best to help you all I can.' Daniel was so good at helping the king that it wasn't long before he was put in charge of everyone else.

Show the picture of Mr Mean and ask if anyone can tell you which Mr Man it is. Allow two or three children to give you an answer.

Yes, it's Mr Mean. When Daniel was alive it was just like today – there were some nice people around but there were also some mean people too. The mean people didn't like Daniel being the king's favourite and so they plotted against him.

Show the picture of the people plotting.

These mean people discussed Daniel and talked about how they might get rid of him. They said things like, 'How are we going to get rid of Daniel? He is far too honest for my liking, so we can never make any money on the side. He never says or does anything wrong. Probably the only way we can get Daniel into trouble is if we think up something to do with his God, the God of the Bible.'

Show the picture of Daniel praying.

You see, Daniel loved God – the true God of the Bible. Every day, three times a day, Daniel would pray and thank God for helping him. But not everyone believed in Daniel's God.

Show the picture of the statue.

Many people believed in and worshipped so-called gods made of stone, wood or clay. Daniel knew there was no point in putting your trust in an object. How could something made by man ever help you in times of trouble? That would be a bit like this. . .

Take the small piece of carved wood or chess piece out of your pocket and start 'praying' to it.

. . .'Oh, little piece of wood, little piece of wood, I have got so many worries and so many problems – will you help me?' (*This obviously looks ridiculous and the children will laugh, but at the same time they get the point about how futile it is to pray to a man-made object.*)

So the people came up with a plan.

Show the picture of King Darius.

They went to see the king and said, 'King Darius, you are such a great king that we think you should have all the people pray to you for the next 30 days. Also, if anyone is caught praying to any other god, anyone other than you, they must be thrown to the lions!' 'What a good idea!' said King Darius – who felt rather flattered – and he gave the order at once.

Show the picture of Daniel praying, being watched.

These mean men knew that Daniel would take no notice of an order that would stop him praying to God, and they went to spy on him. As soon as they saw Daniel praying, they shouted, 'Arrest that man! Take him to the king!'

Show the picture of the unhappy King Darius.

'King Darius,' they said, 'we caught Daniel praying to his God, and you passed a law that anyone caught praying to any god other than you must be thrown to the lions!'

The king was absolutely horrified. He had forgotten how much Daniel loved his God, and he now realised that this had all been a trick to get Daniel into trouble. He was really angry with these mean men but, even though he was the king and the most powerful person in the land, he couldn't think of any way he could save Daniel. He tried pleading with the men, but they would have none of it. 'No, Your Majesty, you made the order and you can't go back on it. The order must stand. Daniel has got to be thrown to the lions!' They laughed to themselves and really thought that this would be the end of Daniel now.

Show the picture of the king and Daniel outside the lions' den.

As Daniel was lowered into the lions' den, King Darius called out to him, 'I hope the God you worship and pray to is able to help you, because I can't!' A big stone was rolled over the entrance, and all went quiet.

Show the picture of Mr Worry and ask if anyone can tell you which Mr Man it is. Allow two or three children to give you an answer.

Yes, this is Mr Worry. You see, the king was now a worried man.

Show the picture of the king in bed.

In fact, he was so worried that he went to bed without any tea and stayed awake all night worrying about Daniel. Would Daniel's God really be able to keep him safe from the lions?

In the morning the king scrambled out of bed and ran as fast as he could to the lions' den. He gave the order for the stone to be removed and he peered in, frightened at what he might find.

Show picture of Daniel in the den.

As he looked in, what do you think he saw? There was Daniel, unhurt and praying to his God! As soon as Daniel saw King Darius, he called up, 'Look, King Darius, I'm safe! My God sent an angel to keep the mouths of the lions shut. I don't even have a scratch!'

Show the picture of Daniel and the king.

King Darius had Daniel pulled out of the lions' den and gave him a great big hug. He was so pleased to see that no harm had come to his friend Daniel. He was also still very angry at the mean men who had tried to get rid of Daniel and the king wasted no time in having these nasty men arrested. Do you know what he did with them?

Allow two or three children to give you an answer.

Yes – they were thrown to the lions. But they were not kept safe – they were all killed.

Daniel was very glad that he had put his trust in God. And King Darius was so pleased that Daniel was OK, that he gave an order that everyone in the land should trust in Daniel's God. Daniel continued to serve and help King Darius, and they both ended up like this Mr Man.

Put up the picture of Mr Happy and ask if anyone can tell you which Mr Man it is. If you cup your ear as you do when gesturing to people to speak up, the children will take this as a signal that it's OK to call out. It brings the assembly talk to a nice end as they all call out 'Mr Happy!'

Yes, Mr Happy. The Bible teaches that when we put our trust in God, things will always work out for the best in the end.

SUGGESTED SONGS:
Be still (13)
God is good (56)
If I go climbing (105)

SUGGESTED PRAYER:
Dear Father, the Bible teaches that you will never leave me, nor will you forsake me. Help me to put my trust in you and to know that when I am afraid I can always call to you for help. Amen.

DAVID AND GOLIATH

VALUE: Courage

BIBLE REFERENCE: 1 Samuel 17

TEACHING POINT: We can rely on God to help us overcome our fears.

NOTES: Before you start your assembly, hide the ping-pong ball with a little piece of double-sided tape attached in a convenient place near the OHP. When you talk about the stone hitting Goliath, stick the ping-pong ball to 'Goliath's' forehead. If the timing is done correctly, it always gets everyone laughing and helps to make the assembly memorable. Instructions are provided for the use of a sketch-board – the ladder letter words are underlined.

YOU WILL NEED: Small step-ladder, helmet, fake beard, fake spear (made from black plastic piping with cardboard top cut to the shape of a spear and covered with silver foil), ping-pong ball with small piece of double-sided sticky tape attached, prepared sketch-board and paints, PowerPoint or OHP acetate and pens (see introductory section on ladder lettering or visit **www.canicholls.com** and **www.childrensministry.co.uk** for information on how to purchase downloads).

I wonder whether you think you are <u>WEAK OR</u> if you think you are <u>STRONG</u>, or somewhere in between?

Often we think that strength has to do with how big someone is – for example, the wrestlers, strong men and weight-lifters that you see on the telly. If you were in a room full of Sumo wrestlers, you probably wouldn't feel very strong, would you? I know I wouldn't feel very strong!

But sometimes we can look at other people, and then look at ourselves, and make a big mistake about who is strong and who is weak.

I'm going to tell you a famous story from the Old Testament part of the Bible. One thousand years before Jesus was born, two armies were preparing to fight each other: the Israelites. . .

Indicate half the children.

. . .over here, you can be the Israelites, and the Philistines. . .

Indicate the other half of the children.

. . .over there, you can be the Philistines.

In the Philistine army there was a gigantic man who was nearly 3 metres tall. His name was Goliath.

Now, I need a volunteer to come out and be Goliath.

Choose a child from the Philistine group and, if possible, have appropriate props such as helmet, bushy beard, 'spear', etc. (As the child gets dressed up, stand in front of him/her so the other children don't see the effect until you want them to. It creates a surprise if you do it that way, and the response is so much better.) Get 'Goliath' to stand on a small step-ladder – ensuring that there is something to hold onto.

Goliath had huge muscles!

Get 'Goliath' to flex his muscles.

He was covered from head to toe in shiny armour, and he carried a massive spear. He was a real show-off. He swaggered about in front of the Israelite army and taunted them. He said, 'You send one of your soldiers to fight me. If he wins, we will all surrender to you. But if I win, you must all surrender to me!' He was quite sure he would win. All the Israelites were terrified of Goliath.

Ask the Israelite group to show you how frightened they can look.

No one had the bottle to go and fight him.

Help 'Goliath' down from the steps and ask him to look all proud and pleased with himself. Then get him to sit on a chair to one side. 'I will call you, Mr Goliath, when I need you.'

There aren't too many 3-metre giants around today – at least I haven't seen any. But we do have some giants in our lives. I'd like to introduce you to one of them now.

Draw in frightening face.

Can you guess what he is called?

Ask two or three of the children to have a guess.

His name is <u>FEAR</u>. There may be things in our lives that frighten us. For example, some people don't like the dark or spiders.

Be careful here, as some children are likely to go off into enthusiastic conversation about what scares them! (See introductory section on keeping control.)

Back to our story. Visiting the Israelite army was a shepherd boy called David. He had only gone there to deliver sandwiches to his older brothers who were soldiers. When David saw Goliath, he thought, 'Oo-er! Look at the size of him!' But when he heard Goliath calling out, he said, 'Who does this guy think he is? I'll go and fight him. I know that God will help me.'

Draw stick-man.

Well, his brothers thought that was hilarious. They made fun of David: 'What? A skinny little thing like you? Don't be daft! You don't know what you're talking about. Run home and play! Go back to your sheep!' They thought that because David didn't look strong, it meant he must be weak.

Draw the cross.

Later on in the New Testament of the Bible, you can read the account of when Jesus was dying on the cross. Jesus seemed so weak hanging there. And people made fun of him too. They said, 'If you're the Son of God, why don't you save yourself?' He could have done – but he didn't. The Bible teaches that he hung there for six long hours until he died, and he did that so that all the wrong things we do in our lives today can be forgiven by God. That must have taken an awful lot of <u>COURAGE</u>. The Bible says that on the night before Jesus was killed, he was very afraid. It's natural to be afraid sometimes. Courage doesn't mean not having any fears. Courage means overcoming your fears.

Back to David. He certainly had courage. He managed to persuade the king to let him go and fight Goliath. Now I need a volunteer to be David.

Select a volunteer from the Israelite group of children to be David. Ask 'Goliath' to stand on the steps again.

When Goliath saw David coming towards him, he roared with laughter. He said, 'I eat little boys like you for breakfast!' He waved his spear in a threatening way.

Get 'Goliath' to wave his spear. Encourage all the other children to gasp with fear.

All David had with him was a sling – a strip of leather with a place at the end to put a stone. David bent down and picked up some stones and placed one in his sling.

Get 'David' to act this out.

He swung it round and round, and then he slung the stone at Goliath. The stone whizzed through the air and hit Goliath right in the middle of his forehead. He fell down with a mighty crash – dead!

Get 'David' and 'Goliath' to act this out. Help 'Goliath' down from the step-ladder, and stick the ping-pong ball to his forehead. Get him to wobble around for a while before falling down.

This means that you, the Israelites, are the winners!

Invite the Israelites to cheer.

Let's give our two actors a big round of applause!

Volunteers sit down.

This was all because David relied on God's <u>POWER</u>.
Three days after Jesus died on the cross, the Bible tells us that God's power. . .

Draw in zap line from POWER to the cross.

. . .raised him from the dead and that he is alive today. Christians believe that if we ask Jesus to be our friend, God will give us his power today. . .

Draw in zap line from POWER to stick man.

. . .not to hurt anyone, but always to help us live good and courageous lives.

Draw in zap line from POWER to COURAGE.

And no matter how small we are, his power can help us to overcome. . .

DRAW a cross through the scary face.

. . . the giant called Fear, and any other giants we may meet along the way – just as his power helped little David to defeat great big Goliath.

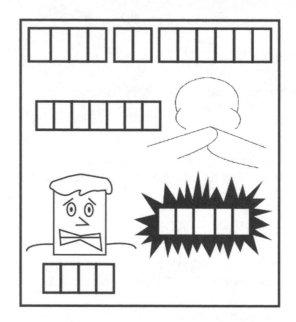

SUGGESTED SONGS:
Be still (13)
Goliath, thump, thump (68)

SUGGESTED PRAYER:
Dear Father, give me your power, not in order that I may hurt anyone, but so I can live a good and courageous life and overcome that giant called Fear. Amen.

DAVID AND KING SAUL

VALUES: Generosity; Honesty; Saying sorry

BIBLE REFERENCES: 1 Samuel 18:1–17, 19:1–10, 24:1–22

TEACHING POINT: Say sorry and ask for forgiveness.

NOTES: Instructions are provided for the use of a sketch-board – the ladder letter words are underlined.

YOU WILL NEED: Prepared sketch-board and paints, PowerPoint or OHP acetate and pens (see introductory section on ladder lettering or visit **www.canicholls.com** and **www.childrensministry.co.uk** for information on how to purchase downloads).

Have you ever felt that you have been blamed for something that wasn't your fault, and because of it you have ended up in big trouble? When that happens you can really feel that you want to get your own back, even if that means doing something wrong yourself.

I want to tell you the story of a person who was <u>TEMPTED</u> to get his own back, but in the end he decided to do the right thing and let God sort it out.

This all happened many years ago when a young man named David became a soldier in King Saul's army. David was a brave soldier and very successful in battle. Everybody liked David and felt safe when he was around. When David and the king marched back into the city where they lived, people would shout out, 'We like King Saul, but we like David even more!' King Saul became extremely jealous.

Talk about jealousy. Ask the children if they have ever been jealous.

Well, King Saul wanted to be <u>TOPS</u> – Number One. He wanted to be everyone's favourite. So he made plans to try and get rid of David. He decided to send him off to fight, secretly hoping he would get killed. But the Bible tells us that God was with David and protected him, and David just became more and more popular. 'What can I do to get rid of him?' thought King Saul. In the end he got really angry. He had such a bad <u>TEMPER</u>.

Talk about anger, especially when we can't get our own way. Ask the children to think about times when they have got angry, and explain that it's at times like these when we can do some really silly things. Give a personal example if you have one that is appropriate.

Back to our story. King Saul was so angry that he tried to kill David with his spear, but David was too quick and dodged out of the way. David realised that it was unsafe to be around King Saul and he decided to get right out of town. He ran away with some of his men into the Desert of En Gedi and hid in a cave. But it wasn't long before somebody split on David and told King Saul where David was hiding. The king took 3,000 men and went after him.

When King Saul and his men reached the Desert of En Gedi, King Saul needed to go to the loo. Now, they didn't have public conveniences in those days so the king went into a cave – and it happened to be the same cave in which David was hiding! It was dark in the cave and the king didn't see David and his men hiding at the back. While the king was 'going to the loo' David's men said, 'Go on David, now's your chance, he can't see you!' David slowly crept up behind King Saul and took out his knife. 'This is my chance to get even!' he thought.

But something inside David was telling him this wasn't right. In a split second he changed his mind and put his <u>TRUST</u> in God's ability to sort things out. He decided only to cut off a corner of the king's cloak. Even after just doing that, David felt really bad. Imagine how he would have felt if he had actually killed the king!

Explain how it takes a lot of courage to do the right thing, especially when it means going against the crowd. Talk about peer pressure. David's men were wanting and expecting him to kill King Saul. David was possibly tempted to kill the king because he was being encouraged by his men. But in the end he decided against it.

King Saul finished 'going to the loo', totally unaware of what had happened. As he walked out of the cave, David followed behind. When the king had gone a little way, David called out to him, 'Look, master. It's not true what people are saying about me.' The king turned round. 'Is that you David?' 'Yes it's me.' And he held up the piece of cloak he'd cut off. 'I could have killed you back there in the cave, but I didn't want any harm to come to you. I care about you. What people have been saying about me wanting to hurt you is just not true.'

When David had finished speaking, King Saul felt really ashamed of himself and asked David to forgive him for being so nasty, so they could be friends again. It's not always easy to own up that we are in the wrong, but we always feel better inside when we admit to the <u>TRUTH</u> about ourselves.

At this point, talk about the Bible teaching that God has given us a conscience. As you do this, draw in the cross.

The Bible teaches that many years later, just like David, Jesus knew what it was like to be blamed for something he didn't do. In fact, it was even worse for Jesus because he was killed, even though he was completely innocent. The Bible teaches, and Christians believe, that Jesus was punished by God, by being nailed to a cross, for all the things that other people have done wrong – people all over the world, and down through the ages. The Bible teaches that God did that so we can be forgiven and live with him for ever.

But, like King Saul, before we can be forgiven we too have to come to a point of admitting that we have done wrong things and say 'sorry' to God and ask for his forgiveness.

I wonder what you will do?

SUGGESTED SONG:
Jesus cares for me (123)

SUGGESTED PRAYER:
Dear Father in heaven, forgive me for the times when I have been jealous and have allowed that jealousy to turn into anger. Help me not to be like that, and help me to feel pleased for other people when they are successful. Amen.

DEAD OR ALIVE?

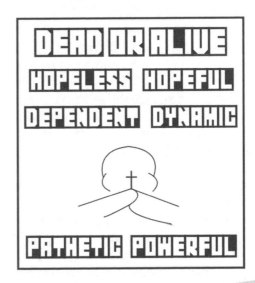

VALUES: Hope; Self-worth

BIBLE REFERENCE: Romans 8:28

TEACHING POINT: Whatever we're like, whatever we do, we're important to God.

NOTES: This assembly is aimed at the older children although the younger ones will always get something from it. I like to use this type of talk at the end of the Summer Term when it is the last time I will be addressing the children going up to secondary school. I feel it re-enforces the reality of God in the world today. Instructions are provided for the use of a sketch-board – the ladder letter words are underlined.

YOU WILL NEED: Prepared sketch-board and paints, PowerPoint or OHP acetate and pens (see introductory section on ladder lettering or visit **www.canicholls.com** and **www.childrensministry.co.uk** for information on how to purchase downloads).

Paint in the title: <u>DEAD OR ALIVE</u>

Have you ever wondered what it would be like to be paralysed from the neck down – only able to move your head? This happened to an American girl, Joni Eareckson *(pronounced 'Johnny Erikson')* in the 1960s when she was 17. She dived into shallow water and broke her neck. Her situation seemed <u>HOPELESS</u>.

In a split second, Joni had gone from being an athletic girl without a care in the world, to being paralysed from the neck down. She had to be suspended in a canvas frame with her head supported by tongs which bit into her flesh. Much later, she was put into a wheelchair. But she couldn't do anything for herself. She was totally <u>DEPENDENT</u>.

Do you think there would be any point in living if that happened to you?

Joni couldn't see any point in living. She became utterly depressed. She couldn't eat and she got dreadfully thin so that in places her bones stuck out through her skin, and she was covered in sores. She had been pretty, but now she was a horrific sight. The first time someone held up a mirror for her, she screamed. Her situation was <u>PATHETIC</u>.

Joni was a Christian, and she asked God many times, *'Why?* Why have you allowed this to happen to me?' She began to try and shut God out of her life.

Then one day she meet a teenager called Steve. Steve loved God and he knew the Bible well, and he helped Joni to see life from God's point of view – from the point of view of eternity. And when Joni thought about eternity – about never-ending life in heaven – then all her concerns about being in a wheelchair became less important.

She still couldn't understand why God had allowed her accident to happen, but now she knew that he would somehow use it for good – that he would weave it into his plan. Things no longer seemed HOPELESS, and Joni became <u>HOPEFUL</u>. There was now an excitement inside Joni. She saw her body like a picture frame. The *really* important thing was the picture *inside* the frame, and she knew God was working on that.

Meanwhile she learnt to draw by holding a pen in her mouth. Her drawings were so good that they soon got noticed and exhibited. Joni became famous, and although she was still DEPENDENT, her life became <u>DYNAMIC</u> – it was full of purpose.

Because of her beautiful drawings, Joni was asked more and more often to speak to groups of people, to give interviews to magazines, and even to be interviewed on radio and television. She always took these opportunities to tell people about her faith. She's also written several books and made a film about her life.

One day, Joni met a bitter young man who'd had both his hands amputated after an accident. He asked her where she got her power from. She told him how having a relationship with Jesus had given her access to God and all his power. She told him that Jesus. . .

Draw a cross.

. . .had died on a cross so that God can forgive us for our sins. When we accept this and give our lives to Jesus, we come into a relationship with God which nothing – not even the greatest tragedy – can ever destroy. The young man with no hands walked away from that meeting transformed.

It's impossible to say how many lives have been changed over the years as a result of Joni telling her story – so you can see that her life, which was once PATHETIC, has turned out to be <u>POWERFUL</u>.

Some people who are young and physically fit think they don't need God. But youth and fitness are temporary things. The difference about life in the kingdom of God, the Bible tells us, is that it is not only powerful but it is everlasting.

I'm sure Joni would be the first person to tell you that you don't have to wait until something awful happens before *you* can have that relationship with God yourself, and be *really* alive, now and for evermore.

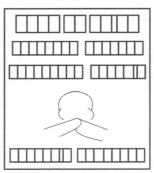

SUGGESTED SONGS:
Early in the morning (39)
If I were a butterfly (107)

SUGGESTED PRAYER:
Dear heavenly Father, please show me how I can take bad situations in my life and turn them around for the good – not just for me, but so that I am able to help others too. Amen.

DRESSING FOR THE OCCASION

VALUES: Courage; Self-worth

BIBLE READING: 1 Samuel 17:38–50

TEACHING POINT: We can do incredible things with God's help.

NOTES: This assembly talk is designed to show children that God can take us as we are and use us to do incredible things. If you have already used the David and Goliath talk which is about overcoming fear, you may wish to start this one by referring to it, and then say there is something else we can learn from the story of David and Goliath.

YOU WILL NEED: Funny/scary mask (obtainable from a novelty shop), large coat, large pair of shoes or boots, pair of oven gloves, length of rope with a knot tied in it, small gift or prize.

This is a story from the Old Testament part of the Bible, and it teaches us something very important. Do any of you know the story of David and Goliath? (Do you remember me telling you the story of David and Goliath?) *Recap briefly here if necessary.*

Well, even though David was much smaller than Goliath he was still able, with the help of God, to beat Goliath in battle. What you may not know is that before David fought Goliath, he went to see King Saul to ask his permission. King Saul said, 'Yes, if you want to, but try this on first.' He started to dress David in his own suit of armour and he put his own bronze helmet on David's head. David then fastened on the king's sword over the armour and started walking around trying to get used to it all.

King Saul was a lot bigger than David and the armour was big and heavy. David said, 'I can't go and fight in all this gear because I'm not used to it.' He took it all off and went to fight Goliath in his normal clothes – a tunic and his sandals. You see, David was a shepherd boy and he had never worn heavy armour before. The only weapon David had ever used was a sling – a strip of leather with a place at the end to put a stone. With his sling he would scare away wild animals when they tried to attack his sheep.

Now, what we can learn from this, girls and boys, is the importance of not trying to be someone you are not. King Saul thought he knew best. He believed that David should go into battle dressed just how he or his best soldiers would have dressed. But David was wise and he quickly realised he had a better chance of surviving if he was just himself.

In life we face all sorts of battles.

Ask the children if they know what you mean. Explain briefly about physical difficulties, the ones you can see, and then about inner difficulties, the ones you can't see but know they exist.

When we have to fight one of life's battles, we can allow other people to influence us and tell us what we should do. Some people give very good advice, but sometimes we can listen to the wrong advice. David was successful because he trusted God. If he had done what King Saul was suggesting, he wouldn't have won his fight. It wasn't that King Saul wanted David to get hurt, but his ideas could have cost David his life.

I spend a lot of time reading my Bible and I have never known God give me wrong advice. I also know that he loves me and can use me just as I am – which is, after all, the way he made me. I haven't got to pretend to be anything or anyone I am not. Let me see if I can show you what I mean. I need someone to help me. Who likes dressing up?

Select a volunteer and ask his/her name.

Now, just imagine you need some extra money, and someone who you think is a friend tells you to steal it. Inside, you may be feeling really worried because you know it's wrong to steal, and you don't want to do it. Of course, you might say, 'No way!' – and that would be the really brave thing to do. But just suppose you didn't want your friend to think you were scared – what might you do then? You might put on a brave face to make out you're not bothered. Here you are [*name*] – can you put on a brave face for me, please?

Get the child to put on the funny/scary mask.

This might look funny, but often we wear our face like a mask to hide our true feelings. If we continue to try and protect our true feelings, we can end up becoming what is known as thick-skinned. Some people might say hard-hearted. Now [*name*] – try this for size!

Get the child to put on the large coat.

That's better! Nothing is going to hurt your feelings now! And what about all those adverts on the telly and in magazines? We have got to have the latest fashion. If we don't, people will laugh at us. We don't want that, do we? Now, here you are [*name*] – try on the latest shoes!

Give the child the large pair of shoes or boots.

Well, you're really looking good! But what about your hands? I think you should have some plastic surgery. That's the thing to have these days. And then you'll need these to protect your new hands.

Give the child the oven gloves to put on.

Give [*name*] a big round of applause. Now he/she is ready to take on the world! I'd like to thank you for being a great help and, before you go and sit down, I would like to say 'thank you' by giving you a prize. But before I do that, there is just one little thing I would like you to do. Could you untie the knot in this piece of rope for me, please?

Give the child the rope and ask him/her to untie the knot whilst still wearing all the attire. This will obviously be impossible to do, and will cause much merriment. After a few moments, ask the child to hand you the rope and take off the garments. Then hand the rope back to the child.

Do you think it will be easier now?

The child will now be able to untie the knot. Give him/her the prize, and ask the children to give your helper another round of applause as he/she sits down.

Can you imagine what it would be like for [name] if he/she'd had to spend the rest of the day wearing all those things? It would be really difficult to do all the things that have to be done throughout the day, wouldn't it?

[Name] looked funny, but there are people who walk around for years pretending to be someone they are not, and usually it's all to cover up what is really going on inside. On the inside they are carrying all sorts of worries and fears that weigh them down. But God never meant us to live life like that. The Bible teaches that nothing is hidden from God. The Bible says that 'Man looks at the outward appearance, but God looks at the heart.' God sees everything.

The Bible also teaches that Jesus wants us to be free from anything that is false, and that if we ask him to be our friend, he will set us free. One thing I have found as a Christian is that as long as I am doing things God's way, I never have to worry about what other people might think of me. And that has enabled me to win many of life's battles, both large and small, and achieve things I never thought possible.

SUGGESTED SONGS:
Be bold, be strong (11)
Goliath, thump, thump (68)
My God is so big (157)

SUGGESTED PRAYER:
Help me, Father, not to be afraid of being the person you created me to be, and help me to realise that with you I can do incredible things. Amen.

FAILURE NEED NEVER BE FINAL

VALUE: Aiming high

BIBLE REFERENCE: Romans 3:23

TEACHING POINT: We can't be perfect, but God will forgive us if we ask him to.

NOTES: Instructions are provided for the use of a sketch-board – the ladder letter words are underlined.

YOU WILL NEED: Velcro magnetic dartboard and 'darts' (which can be purchased from toy shops like Early Learning Centre); prepared sketch-board and paints, PowerPoint or OHP acetate and pens (see introductory section on ladder lettering or visit **www.canicholls.com** and **www.childrensministry.co.uk** for information on how to purchase downloads).

One of the things we all worry about in life is <u>FAILURE</u>. Getting things wrong.

When I was very young, I can remember doing my sums and sometimes I would do something like this: 1 + 2 = <u>5</u>. What do you think my teacher did? Yes, that's right, my teacher did this. . .

Draw 'X' by the sum.

It's not far out, so couldn't my teacher have put a tick? No, because even though I was only two out, I had failed to get the answer right.

Write the answer in correctly and put in a tick.

I want to tell you something about failure, and it's this. Failure need never be final, as long as you don't give up. Did you know that a man called Albert Einstein failed a maths test when he was at school, but he went on to become one of the world's greatest scientists? Some people give up as soon as things get difficult – but Albert Einstein didn't.

OK, let's try something else. Let's have a spelling competition. I will go first. I will write a word and you can see just how good I am.

Write TREA.

There you are, girls and boys, see how good I am at spelling the word 'tree'!

Carry on praising yourself as though nothing is wrong. The children will be shouting out and telling you that you have spelt the word incorrectly. Don't let this go on for too long. Eventually you realise your mistake, draw in the <u>X</u> and say. . .

Well, it's only one letter out – does it really matter? *Let the children respond.* Yes it does, doesn't it? Let me put it right.

Write in TREE *and a tick.*

OK, let's have a sports competition. Let's play darts! I need someone to come and throw some darts at my dartboard. Who is going to have a go?

Select a child.

The only thing is, to win you have to hit the bull's-eye every time!

Give the child the three 'darts' and ask him/her to stand several feet away from the dartboard. Obviously the child will not be able to achieve what you are asking for. Let two or three more children have a go, depending on the time available – and always make sure that each child is given a big round of applause for having a go. Finish by picking one of the older children, or even a teacher, just to emphasise the point that it is impossible, no matter who we are.

The Bible teaches that God has a standard of how he wants us to behave. But God's standard is so high that it is impossible to reach – just like it is impossible to hit the bull's-eye every time. We might achieve it once, we might even achieve it twice, but we can never achieve it every time. And we only have to go slightly wrong, like I did with my sum and my spelling, and we have failed.

When we fail to reach God's standard, the Bible calls it <u>SIN</u>. And sin stops me from having a relationship with God. So what can be done? If I want to be friends with God, it means that I have got to get things absolutely right every time, and that is just impossible. But remember what I said? 'Failure need never be final.'

You see, God knew that we would never be able to get it right every time, and so he had a plan to help us. Let me explain. Put your hand up if you have ever told a lie. *(Pause)* Put your hand up if you have ever done anything you know you shouldn't have done. *(Pause)* Put your hand up if you have ever been punished for doing something naughty. *(Pause)*

Well, the Bible teaches that God punishes sin, but he loves us so much that 2,000 years ago. . .

Draw the cross.

. . .he sent his Son, Jesus, to die on a cross to take the blame for every time we get it wrong – not for sums or spelling of course, but for not reaching his perfect standard in everything we think and say and do. He sent Jesus to live on this earth for a while, and Jesus was the only one who *did* reach God's standard every day.

So when we ask Jesus to be our friend, the Bible says that God forgives us for all the times we have got it wrong. And. . .

Place one of the 'darts' on the bull's-eye.

. . .it's like hitting the bull's-eye every time!

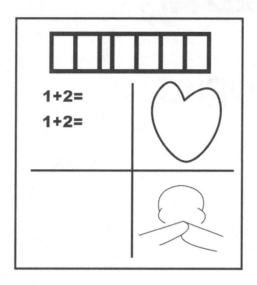

SUGGESTED SONGS:
For all have sinned (46)
Jesus cares for me (123)

SUGGESTED PRAYER:
Dear Father in heaven, forgive me when I fall short of your standard.
Thank you for sending Jesus to die for me and for making it possible
for me to get things right with you. Amen.

FIREWORKS

VALUES: Love; Patience; Respect

BIBLE REFERENCE: 2 Corinthians 4:16–18

TEACHING POINT: People are all different and that is good.

NOTES: This is a talk which can be adapted to suit different styles. Here the talk is presented by asking questions and writing down the children's answers. However, if you happen to have artistic flair, you could paint large and colourful fireworks in cartoon-style onto separate pieces of card, and cut a hole through which a child could put his/her face. Volunteers would then stand and hold the cards with their heads poking through whilst you were speaking. This would make for much fun and really bring the talk alive visually.

YOU WILL NEED: board, or OHP acetate and pens, fireworks on card (as in 'Notes' above – optional).

Who likes fireworks? What is your favourite firework?

Brainstorm answers onto a blank acetate or board. Add some names of your own if necessary.

If you want a really first rate fireworks display, you need a good variety of different kinds of fireworks. And in a first rate school, you need a good variety of different kinds of people.

Now, fireworks remind me of certain kinds of people:

- Some people are like *Bangers* – they're quick to say what they think, sometimes they even shout what they think, and they can make you jump if you're of a nervous disposition!
- Some people are like *Rockets* – they're confident and they get noticed because they always seem to be doing important things.
- Some people are like *Roman Candles* – they're gentle people who just get on with things in their own quiet way, and you can always rely on them.
- Some people are like *Catherine Wheels* – they lead very busy lives and have loads of energy, and they usually seem to be in a flat spin!
- And some people are like *Sparklers* – these are home-loving people who don't want to do anything spectacular like climbing mountains or parachuting, but when you're with them they cheer you up and make you feel better.

Wouldn't it be boring – and deafening! – if you went to a fireworks display composed entirely of 'Bangers'! Or all 'Catherine Wheels'. Or all 'Rockets'. Pretty unimaginative.

It's the same in this school, and it's the same everywhere. If we were all the same it would be very boring. The Bible tells us that God has created us on purpose to be different from each other, so that each one of us has got a different part of God's own character within us. We don't always see each other like that, do we? It means, of course, that no matter what we're like, we're all equally necessary and equally special, and we all need each other.

What are some of the words you could use to describe fireworks?

Brainstorm again and add adjectives of your own if necessary.

- Pretty
- Exciting
- Dangerous

- Expensive
- Temporary

A firework is one of the most temporary things in existence. How many seconds does a rocket last?

But actually, everything we can see around us is temporary. Houses are temporary, cars are temporary, our bodies are temporary, and in the end even the planets and the stars in the universe are temporary. And of course our *troubles* are temporary too.

If you think about eternity – for ever and ever without end – then our lives on this earth are as fleeting as fireworks. A quick burst of activity – maybe very spectacular – and then we fizzle out.

But the Bible tells us that God's love is eternal – it lasts for ever – and that God longs to have a loving relationship with you and me. That's why he sent his Son, Jesus, to die on a cross so that, when we ask Jesus to be our friend, God is able to forgive us for all the bad things we've done. Then, the Bible tells us, we can have a loving relationship with God that will last for ever and ever without end.

God also wants us to have a loving relationship with each other. And it's his love that enables us to do this – that enables a 'Roman Candle' to get on with a 'Banger', and a 'Rocket' to get on with a 'Sparkler'!

There are lots of different sorts of personalities in this room, and occasionally we rub each other up the wrong way. But this is so trivial and silly if you think about it. A hundred years or so from now, it's likely that every one of us in this room today will have gone from this earth. But the Bible tells us that God's love is everlasting, and that when we are willing to accept God's love into our hearts, then that love will shine out from us and will help us to love the people we find difficult to love on our own.

SUGGESTED SONGS:
Father God created the world (42)
God gave me ears (55)
Jesus put this song into our hearts (129)

SUGGESTED PRAYER:
Father, help us to love each other and to be patient with one another, and to remember that when we meet other people who are different from us, that's a good thing. Thank you for the amazing variety of human beings you have created. Amen.

FIVE PLUS TWO EQUALS FIVE THOUSAND

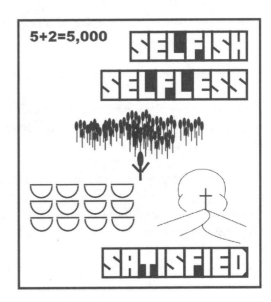

VALUES: Love; Sharing

BIBLE REFERENCES: John 6:1–14; Philippians 4:19

TEACHING POINT: We can trust God to supply our needs.

NOTES: Instructions are provided for the use of a sketch-board – the ladder letter words are underlined.

YOU WILL NEED: Bright red card cut to form a heart shape; prepared sketch-board and paints, PowerPoint or OHP acetate and pens (see introductory section on ladder lettering or visit **www.canicholls.com** and **www.childrensministry.co.uk** for information on how to purchase downloads).

Complete the sum 5 + 2 = <u>5,000</u>, and ask the children if they think this could be possible.

The Bible teaches that nothing is impossible with God! Can anyone tell me what a miracle is?

Thank the children for their definitions and then clarify in your own words.

This is a story from the Bible. Jesus and his twelve disciples had been very busy and they were feeling rather tired, so one day they decided to go out into the countryside to chill out.

Draw an indication of the central group of people, and Jesus in front of them.

But lots of people found out where they were going and followed them, because everyone loved to hear Jesus talk to them.

Add some more colourful dots to the ones already there, to indicate a vast crowd.

Soon there was a crowd of 5,000 people. But Jesus wasn't annoyed.

He talked to them about God, and he told them stories to illustrate what he was saying, and he made ill people better. And everyone was very happy and time flew by – just like it always does when you're having fun!

In no time at all it was teatime, and the people began to feel hungry because they'd rushed off in pursuit of Jesus without thinking about taking any food with them. Jesus felt sorry for them, and he said to Philip, one of his disciples, 'Where shall we buy bread for these people to eat?' Philip said, 'But Jesus that would cost a fortune! And in any case we're miles away from a shop. But even if there was a shop, we haven't got any money!'

The situation seemed hopeless, and everyone looked at Jesus and wondered what he would do. Imagine if you were entertaining 5,000 people at home – what a lot of sandwiches you'd have to make!

But in the crowd there was a young boy whose mum had very sensibly packed him up a picnic. He was starving hungry, but he loved Jesus and he could see that Jesus needed some food to feed the crowd with. He thought to himself, 'I've only got five small loaves and two little fishes – what shall I do?'

Imagine if you'd got a bag of sweets and everyone in the playground wanted one – would you give them *all* away?

The boy had to make a decision: either to eat his picnic himself and be <u>SELFISH</u>, or give his picnic to Jesus. Which do you think he did? Yes, he ran up and gave Jesus the lot. He was <u>SELFLESS</u>.

Explain 'selfless' if necessary.

The Bible teaches that Jesus himself was selfless. . .

Draw cross.

. . . when he died on the cross so that God can forgive us for all the bad things we've done, if we ask him to.

As you can imagine, Jesus was really pleased with the boy. He broke up the five loaves and two fishes into pieces and said to the crowd, 'Sit down on the grass in groups.' He said to the first group, 'Eat all you want!' And it was amazing – there was still some food left over! Then he said to the second group, 'Eat all you want!' And it was extraordinary – there was still some food left over! In the end, all 5,000 people, including the young boy, had eaten all they wanted. And there was *still* some left over!

Afterwards, the disciples gathered up the leftovers. And there wasn't just one basketful of leftovers. . .

Draw the baskets, one by one, as you speak.

. . .or two, or three, or four, or five, or six, or seven, or eight, or nine, or ten, or eleven – but *twelve* basketfuls of leftovers! The Bible says that that's what Jesus could do with just five loaves and two fishes. Everyone was <u>SATISFIED</u>. It was a miracle!

So, it doesn't matter if you're young or if you don't have much. The Bible says that Jesus loves you anyway. And when you share with others, he's pleased. Because small gifts can result in great big miracles.

You don't have to have food or sweets in order to share. There are other things you can share, like your time.

Give an example.

And there is one very special thing that always *increases* if you share it. Can you think what it is?

You can prompt the children if you wish by holding up a bright red heart shape!

Yes, *love*. When you give your love away, you will find lots of love coming back to you. And then you've got even more to give away!

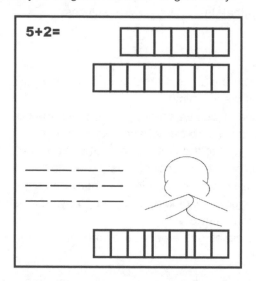

SUGGESTED SONGS:
Father, I place into your hands (44)
If I go climbing (105)
I'm working out what it means (116)

SUGGESTED PRAYER:
Thank you, Father, for caring for me and looking after me. Help me to know that I can always trust you to supply all my needs. Help me also to be willing to share what is mine with others. Amen.

FREE TO CHOOSE

VALUES: Choosing right; Happiness

BIBLE REFERENCE: I Kings 18:20–39; Joshua 24:15

TEACHING POINT: Ask for God's help to make the right choices.

NOTES: Instructions are provided for the use of a sketch-board – the ladder letter words are underlined.

YOU WILL NEED: Prepared sketch-board and paints, PowerPoint or OHP acetate and pens (see introductory section on ladder lettering or visit **www.canicholls.com** and **www.childrensministry.co.uk** for information on how to purchase downloads).

Can anyone tell me what they would like to be when they leave school?

Let two or three children answer.

Here is something that we all want to be: <u>FREE TO CHOOSE</u>.

One of the games I liked to play when I was very young was hide-and-seek. Have you ever played that? You close your eyes and count to 100 while your friends run and hide, and then you go and search for them. It's great fun. I can remember I would often look in all the wrong places first. I can also remember feeling really happy when I found the person I was looking for.

Life can sometimes be like that. People are looking for happiness, but never seem to find it because often they are looking in all the wrong places. I can remember when I was young and I fell in love. She was beautiful!

Make this personal to you as you draw a picture of a face and underneath put the words: <u>POP IDOL</u>. The funnier the face, the better!

Lots of people have pop idols, and it's good that we can be free to choose who we follow. We watch them on the telly, and collect their pictures and CDs or download their songs so we can listen to them whenever we want. We may even spend money on going to see them on stage. But the thing is, pop idols don't last for ever. One minute you will see them on the telly, and the next minute they've disappeared and someone else has taken their place. Some last longer than others, of course, but none of them lasts for ever. No one I know has ever found true happiness in following a pop idol.

Some people choose this to try and find happiness: <u>MONEY</u>.

Draw the £ sign.

Now, there is nothing wrong with money. It's very useful and we all need to have it. Some people say that money is the root of all evil, but that is a misquotation from the Bible. The Bible actually says, 'The *love* of money is the root of all evil.' Some people will do anything to get money. Some people have even killed for money. The more money they get, the more they want, because they are never satisfied. There are two types of people in the world today. There are those who love money and use people, but there are also those who love people and use money. I wonder, which would you rather be?

People will often choose pop idols and money as their gods. What do you think I mean by 'gods'?

Let two or three children respond. If one gets it right, acknowledge the child and then elaborate in your own words.

Yes, a god is anything we put first in our life, and the Bible refers to such things as <u>FALSE GODS</u>.

I want to tell you a story from the Old Testament part of the Bible about a time when there were people following a lot of false gods, and one of these gods was named Baal. There was a man named Elijah who followed the <u>TRUE GOD</u> of the Bible, and he challenged all the people who followed Baal. He said to them, 'Build a big bonfire and put some food on it,' – a bit like an enormous barbeque – 'don't light it, but ask your god, Baal, to light it. After you've done that, I will do the same, except that I will ask *my* God to light it. Whichever god lights the fire is the true God.'

The people who followed Baal accepted the challenge and built a big bonfire and placed some uncooked meat on it and then prayed to their god. 'Oh Baal, answer us! Light our fire!' they cried. But nothing happened. All day long they tried, but nothing.

'OK,' said Elijah, 'now it's my turn.' Elijah built his big bonfire and put some uncooked meat on it. He even poured lots and lots of water over it. Then he prayed to his God, the true God of the Bible. And do you know what?

Draw the flames on the fire.

Fire fell from the sky and it was so fierce that it burnt everything up. Everything was gone – even the water had completely evaporated!

You can go into the story in more detail if you wish. I would do this if I were using the talk for a family service at church, but for schoolchildren, many of whom are un-churched, I tend to keep Bible stories very simple. Never be afraid to use 'artistic licence' if it makes the story easier to understand.

We all have choices to make, and we are all free to choose to follow whoever we like. But I would like to tell you about a choice I made some years ago.

Again you will have to make this personal to you, depending on your own testimony.

I decided not to put my trust in pop idols or money for happiness. Someone told me. . .

Draw in the cross.

. . .about Jesus, and I decided to find out more about him. I found out that Jesus had died so that I could be really happy. What do I mean by that? Well, the Bible teaches, and Christians believe, that we can never be truly happy all the time we are separated from God, the true God of the Bible. It goes on to say that Jesus died on the cross to take the blame for all the bad things that we do which separate us from God. All we need to do is say 'sorry' to God and ask Jesus to be our friend, and then we can have a relationship with God that will last for ever.

Freedom of choice is a good thing, and I can still choose different singers to listen to – people like .... or .... *(use a couple of names that let the children see you haven't lost touch!)*. I enjoy listening to all different types of music. I also choose to earn money so that I can buy the things I need and also buy the things I like.

But the best choice I have ever made in life, and one that I have never been sorry for, was the choice to follow Jesus. Jesus is not like a pop idol, here today and gone tomorrow. And he is not like money, which easily runs out. I have found that Jesus is always there and always ready to help me. And because of that, even when things aren't going so well, I am always truly happy deep down inside.

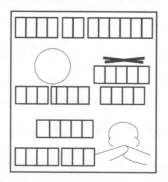

SUGGESTED SONGS:
Hands, hands, fingers, thumbs (76)
I can do all things (97)

SUGGESTED PRAYER:
Dear Father in heaven, please forgive me for the times when I have put other things before you. Thank you that we have freedom to choose, but help me when I am faced with difficult decisions, and give me wisdom to make the right choices. Amen.

GONE FISHING!

VALUES: Obedience; Trust

BIBLE REFERENCE: Luke 5:1–11

TEACHING POINT: Jesus wants us to trust him and be his friend.

NOTES: Instructions are provided for the use of a sketch-board – the ladder letter words are underlined.

YOU WILL NEED: Prepared sketch-board and paints, PowerPoint or OHP acetate and pens (see introductory section on ladder lettering or visit **www.canicholls.com** and **www.childrensministry.co.uk** for information on how to purchase downloads).

Have any of you ever gone fishing? Did you know that some people like fishing so much that they stay out all night trying to catch something? And then there are other people who have to stay out all night, not because they love fishing but because it is their job and that is how they earn their living. It can be extremely hard work.

Draw an unhappy face.

Look at this person. How do you think he is feeling? Yes, he is feeling very down in the dumps. His name is Simon. We can read about Simon in the Bible. After he became friends with Jesus, he changed his name to Peter – but that's another story.

Simon earned his living by catching fish. He had been out all night and had caught absolutely nothing. Not a sausage! Not even a tiddler! So I imagine he was feeling a bit like this.

Indicate unhappy face.

Do you ever feel like that? Life can sometimes make us feel exactly like that. We can work really hard at something, and then it all seems to go wrong or come to nothing. Well, the Bible teaches that God cares about our feelings and he doesn't want us to feel all down in the dumps.

Simon was sitting on the beach cleaning his nets when he saw a large crowd following someone. Who do you think it might be?

Let a couple of the children have a guess, and then draw in the cross.

Yes, it was Jesus. All the people gathered round to listen to Jesus. They loved listening to him. The things he said and the stories he told just seemed to make sense. Well, this day there was such a large crowd that Jesus couldn't see everyone properly. So he said to Simon, 'May I borrow your boat for a while, please? There's such a large crowd that it will be easier to speak to them if I can stand in your boat a little way out from the shore.' 'No problem!' said Simon. 'Get into the boat and I will push you out a little way.' Jesus got into the boat and Simon pushed it out just enough so that Jesus could see everyone.

After Jesus had finished speaking to the people, he said to Simon, 'It looks as though you didn't have a very good catch last night!' 'No, it was awful,' said

Simon. 'I tell you what,' said Jesus. 'Go out again into the deep water.' Simon started to look like this:

Draw a thoughtful face with a question mark.

'But we've been out all night long, Jesus, and we've caught absolutely nothing,' said Simon.

There are times when we can be like that. We question Jesus. The Bible is full of instructions about how we should live and how we should love one another. The trouble is, many people just don't want to know. They turn their backs on God and refuse to listen to what he says. The Bible calls that 'sin'.

(If you wish, you can go into more detail here about sin and its consequences, in a way that is relevant to the age group.)

I wonder what Simon will do – will he listen to Jesus? Well, he thought for a minute and then he said, 'OK Jesus, if you say so.' What Simon was doing was deciding to put his trust in Jesus and not in his own understanding. Secretly I expect he was thinking, 'This is absolutely pointless!' Many people feel that following Jesus is a pointless exercise.

Simon and his brother took their boat out again into deep water and let down the nets. And they couldn't believe it! The nets were so full of fish that they had trouble pulling them in. In fact, they had to call out to the other fishermen to come and help. It was incredible! There were so many fish that the boat nearly sank.

Do you think that Simon was pleased now? Yes! But if he had not done what Jesus said, he would still be feeling miserable and fed up, wouldn't he?

Simon now knew that there was something special about Jesus. A strange feeling came over him as he began to realise just who Jesus was. He started to think of all the naughty things he had done in the past, and he felt unclean on the inside. 'I don't deserve to have a friend like you, Jesus. You shouldn't even come near someone like me.'

What do you think Jesus said to Simon then?

Let one or two children give you an answer.

Jesus said to Simon that he wanted him to be his special friend and help him to teach other people about God. And do you know what Simon did? He immediately left his boat and his nets – everything he had – so that he could follow Jesus.

The Bible teaches, and Christians believe, that Jesus wants *us* to be his special friends and to give up anything that stops us from following him – especially bad thoughts, bad words and bad deeds. He knows that those things will never make us happy. He wants us to be like Simon and put our trust in him and do the things he tells us to. If we do, he knows we will end up like this:

Draw a smiling face.

SUGGESTED SONGS:
Father God, I wonder (43)
I will make you fishers of men (103)
Jesus is my Saviour (126)

SUGGESTED PRAYER:
Dear heavenly Father, please guide me this day. Help me to stop doing anything that prevents me from following Jesus, and help me to remember that I can always put my trust in you. Amen.

GUESS THE PRICE

VALUES: Peace; Self-worth

BIBLE REFERENCE: John 3:16

TEACHING POINT: We are all important and priceless to God.

NOTES: Instructions are provided for the use of a sketch-board – the ladder letter words are underlined.

YOU WILL NEED: Three to four items which will be familiar and interesting to the children and of which you know the value; prepared sketch-board and paints, PowerPoint or OHP acetate and pens (see introductory section on ladder lettering or visit **www.canicholls.com** and **www.childrensministry.co.uk** for information on how to purchase downloads).

Hold up the three or four items and ask the children to guess their value.

One more question. What do you think I am worth? One way to find out would be to look in my bank account to see how much <u>MONEY</u> I have.

There is a fascination these days to know what people are worth. Every year one of the newspapers publishes a 'Rich List'. To get onto that list, you have to be worth millions of pounds. Someone like me would never get onto that list, because I don't have much in the bank compared with a millionaire.

Sometimes a person's bank statement tells them that they are what is called 'overdrawn'. Can anyone explain what I mean by overdrawn? I will give you a clue.

Draw a negative (minus) sign as the horizontal of the cross. Let two or three children have a guess, and then you can explain in more detail.

Yes, being overdrawn is when I have spent more money than I have got in my bank account. There are times when my bank will let me do this – they will agree an overdraft limit. They will say, 'You can go this far, but no further.' If I go over that limit, I am punished by being charged a fee, and eventually I have to pay the price. I can then find myself getting deeper into debt. Debt is a really worrying problem for many people, and they need special help to get out of their difficulties.

Turn the minus sign into a plus sign.

Have you ever been punished for doing something you shouldn't have done? Do you think it's fair when people get punished for doing wrong – robbing banks, for example?

Well, the Bible teaches that God punishes sin. Can anyone tell me the meaning of the word 'sin'?

Let two or three children have a guess, acknowledge and thank them for their answers, and then elaborate in your own words – i.e. bad thoughts, bad words, bad deeds, etc.

Sin is like having a huge debt that we can't pay back, and we need special help to get rid of the problem.

Another way of looking at what I am worth is this: <u>ME</u>.

What is the value of 'me'? We can compare ourselves with others. For example, if I were a famous person that you saw on the telly, a company might pay me a vast amount of money to advertise a product like trainers. They would never do that with someone who was unknown. We may look at someone on the telly and think that person is more valuable than us, or more important than us. What we are really doing is putting too low a value on ourselves just because we aren't famous.

Maybe someone has called you names and has hurt your feelings. When that happens, you can end up feeling absolutely worthless. Then you are letting other people put a low value on you.

Others might not think that you are especially valuable, and *you* might not think you are especially valuable. But according to God you are <u>PRICELESS</u>. The Bible teaches that 'God so loved the world (that means each of you) that he gave his only Son – Jesus. . .

Elongate the vertical line of the plus sign to make it obvious that you are now referring to the cross of Christ.

. . .so that anyone who believes in him should not perish, but have eternal life.'

When Jesus died on the cross, your debt with God was <u>PAID</u>. The Bible teaches that Jesus died for you, and that makes you a very special person. The Bible teaches that all we need to do is accept God's gift of forgiveness by asking Jesus to be our friend.

Another way of putting a value on ourselves is <u>MATERIAL</u>. Here's an interesting question: what is my *body* worth? Well, there are some clever scientists who have worked it out. We have enough iron in our body to make a nail, enough fat to make about seven bars of soap, enough calcium to whitewash a small shed, and enough water to fill two or three buckets. There are a few more things that I can't remember, but all-in-all you're worth about £10, if that!

So, you might not have a lot of money and so you might not feel very rich. Other people, and those scientists, might not think you are very valuable. But that is only looking at life through the world's eyes. Christians believe that if you start to look at life through God's eyes, you will see things in a much more positive way. You will see that because of Jesus, you can get out of debt with God, and you will see that you are of tremendous value. When you start to realise that, you will start to get a lot of this: <u>PEACE</u>.

Peace of heart and peace of mind. You can't get it by being famous and you can't get it by being rich. But peace is something that everyone wants. And they could have it . . . *(point to the cross)* . . . if only they knew where to look.

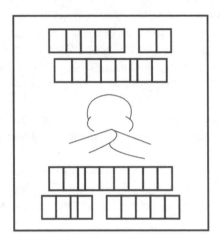

SUGGESTED SONGS:
Father God created the world (42)
If I were a butterfly (107)

SUGGESTED PRAYER:
Dear Father in heaven, please forgive me for the times I have made others feel small by saying things in order to hurt their feelings. Help me also to forgive others when I am hurt by them. You proved by sending your Son, Jesus, just how important and priceless we all are to you, and for that we are for ever grateful. Amen.

GUESS WHO'S COMING TO DINNER

VALUE: Thoughtfulness

BIBLE REFERENCE: Luke 14:16–24

TEACHING POINT: We need to make time for Jesus.

NOTES: You will notice that I have slightly altered the words of this story (using artistic licence) to enable the children to connect with it a little more easily. The message, however, remains the same. Instructions are provided for the use of a sketch-board – the ladder letter words are underlined.

YOU WILL NEED: A balloon prepared by blowing it up, drawing a face on it, letting it down and putting it in your pocket ready for when you need it; prepared sketch-board and paints, PowerPoint or OHP acetate and pens (see introductory section on ladder lettering or visit **www.canicholls.com** and **www.childrensministry.co.uk** for information on how to purchase downloads).

I wonder if you have ever had one of these? <u>INVITATION</u>.

This is a story Jesus told to explain something about the kingdom of heaven. I have changed the wording a little bit just to bring it up to date, but it goes something like this.

Once upon a time there was a rich man who wanted to have a big dinner party. He made a guest list and sent his servant out to invite those people.

But the first person said, 'I have just bought a house and I need to do some DIY on it, so I haven't got time to come. Give your master my apologies.'

And the second person said, 'I have just bought a horse and I want to ride it this evening to try it out, so I haven't got time to come. Give your master my apologies.'

And the third person said, 'I've just got married, and my wife and I want a quiet evening in together. Give your master my apologies.'

And all the other people on the list made excuses too. Have you ever made an excuse to get out of doing something?

Allow the children to respond.

When the servant reported back that none of the people on the list had accepted the invitation, his master was very angry. He said to his servant, 'OK then, go into the streets and collect everyone who is homeless or lonely or hungry, and bring *them* to my dinner party instead!' So that is what the servant did.

Just imagine, girls and boys! You're feeling lonely and down in the dumps, and then someone suddenly invites you to a party and you discover that all your favourite food is on the table! I suspect that the people who were invited first began to wish that *they* had accepted the invitation – but now it was too late.

Draw in the sad face.

What do you think the dinner party represents in the story, girls and boys? Have you any ideas?

Allow some children to respond.

Yes, Jesus was talking about the kingdom of heaven, and he was saying that it's like a great big party to which we are invited.

The people who were originally invited to the party were <u>SELFISH</u>. They only thought about themselves and what *they* wanted to do. Not only were they selfish, they were also <u>SILLY</u>. They could have gone to the party and had a great time, and done all the other things another day, couldn't they?

Now, what do you think this means? <u>RSVP</u>.

Allow the children to respond, and explain if necessary.

'RSVP' stands for some French words which in English mean 'Reply If You Please'. When a person sends you an invitation they would like to know if you are going to be there. This is an invitation to all of us, and so I am going to put your name here: <u>YOU</u>.

Draw in the cross.

The Bible teaches that Jesus came into this world to teach us about God and to make it possible for us to live with him for ever in heaven, by dying for us on the cross. We accept God's invitation to heaven by realising our need for forgiveness, and accepting Jesus as our friend.

The second group of people in the story – the homeless and poor people – were <u>STARVING</u>. They couldn't wait to get to the feast and enjoy all the goodies. Not only that, most importantly of all, they got to know the rich man and realised their lives would never be the same again. They were <u>SAVED</u>. So who do those people represent? They represent every person in the world who knows that he or she needs help from God and is willing to accept that help.

When we realise our need for forgiveness and accept God's invitation to heaven by asking Jesus to be our friend, then we know that our lives are never going to be the same again. Because the kingdom of heaven isn't just somewhere we go to when we die. It begins here on earth, the Bible tells us, the moment we accept the invitation.

Blow up the balloon with the face drawn on it.

But if we're just too busy getting what *we* want out of life to be bothered with God's invitation, one day we could find – like the first group of people in the story – that it's too late. Because, sooner or later, time runs out on us all.

Slowly allow the air to escape from the balloon.

At that time, the Bible tells us, the people who have accepted the invitation will be welcomed into the best party you could possibly imagine.

Draw in the happy face.

And what's more – it will never end!

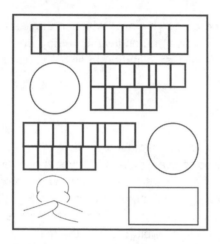

HE IS ABLE TO SAVE

VALUES: Courage; Trust

BIBLE REFERENCES: Matthew 14:22–33; Hebrews 7:25

TEACHING POINT: With Jesus around, we need never be afraid.

NOTES: This particular approach suits my style – and possibly yours. As the puppet interrupts me, I pretend to be surprised and slightly annoyed at the intrusion, as if the puppet has caught me off guard and confused me. I get a lot of laughs from the children with this, but at the same time I am able to communicate the point that with Jesus around, everything is going to work out well in the end.

YOU WILL NEED: A ventriloquist's puppet.

YOU	It had been a very busy day for Jesus and his friends. Jesus had been telling huge crowds of people about how much God loves and cares for them. He had also spent time making the sick people feel better. It was now the end of the day and everyone was feeling tired. It was time to go home.
	Jesus said to his twelve special friends, 'You get in the boat and go across to the other side of the lake, and I will catch up with you later.' So that is what they did. I just want you to picture the scene – they've got lots to talk about and there they are getting into the boat.
PUPPET	I say!
YOU	What do you say?
PUPPET	One's just lost his welly!
YOU	What do you mean, one has just lost his welly?
PUPPET	It fell in the water!
YOU	What do you mean, it fell in the water?
PUPPET	Well you said picture the scene, and I just pictured one losing his welly!
YOU	How could he lose his welly? They didn't wear wellies. Anyway, don't interrupt me! I'm trying to tell the girls and boys a story. As I was saying, there they were getting into the boat, and they started to row out across the lake. As they were rowing, do you know what happened, girls and boys?
PUPPET	The sun came out!
YOU	How could the sun come out when it was the end of the day? No, it started to get dark. Not only did it get dark, but the wind started to blow. And it blew, and it blew.
PUPPET	And it yellow and it green!
YOU	What do you mean, and it yellow and it green?
PUPPET	Well you said it blue!
YOU	I know I said it blew.
PUPPET	Well I said it green!
YOU	This has got nothing to do with colours. I'm talking about the wind blowing. There was a storm brewing and the wind was blowing and the sea was beginning to get rough. The waves started coming over the side of the boat. It must have been a really bad storm because these men were used to being in a boat at sea, but in the story it says they got really scared.

Now, Jesus knew his friends would be afraid, and he wanted to be with them. He wanted to let them know that you never have to be afraid when you have God looking after you. Anyway, Jesus did something only he could do.

PUPPET What was that?

YOU Jesus went to his friends walking on the water! When the men in the boat saw someone walking towards them on the water, they didn't know it was Jesus, and they thought they had seen a ghost! They started to shout, 'It's a ghost! It's a ghost! We're all going to die!' That's when Jesus called out, 'Don't be afraid, lads! It's me – it's Jesus!'

Peter shouted back, 'If that's you, Jesus, you tell me to walk on the water like you!' Jesus said, 'OK, you can do it! Come on then, but keep your eyes fixed on me!' Peter put one leg out of the boat – and it was just like treading on the floor! He thought to himself, 'This is a bit of all right – but they'll never believe me back home!' He put the other leg out – and all of a sudden Peter found himself walking on the water, just like Jesus!

But then Peter took his eyes off Jesus and started to look at the size of the waves and listen to how loud the wind was blowing. As he did this, all his confidence and trust in God vanished, and he started to sink. As he started to sink, he called out – what do you think he called out?

PUPPET 'I want my mum!'

YOU No, he called out to Jesus, 'Jesus, Jesus, save me! I'm drowning!' And what do you think Jesus did?

PUPPET Jumped on his head!

YOU No, Jesus would never do a thing like that. Jesus put out his hand to save Peter. As soon as Peter's hand was in the hand of Jesus, he didn't feel scared anymore. And he stopped sinking into the water. And the wind and the waves no longer seemed to be a problem. It wasn't long before Jesus and Peter were safely in the boat. And all the other men felt safe as well – because as soon as Jesus was there, the storm stopped and the boat was able to reach the other side of the lake. As the men were talking to one another, one of them could be heard saying, 'I don't know, whenever Jesus is around, everything just seems to work out all right in the end!'

(To puppet) Did you enjoy that [name of puppet]?

PUPPET   Yes.

YOU   Well, say cheerio to [*name of puppet*], girls and boys, and I'll put him/her back in the case. *(Children say cheerio.)*

PUPPET   Cheerio!

SUGGESTED SONGS:
Be bold, be strong (11)
Because the Lord is with me (14)

SUGGESTED PRAYER:
Thank you, Father, that you are always in control, and that with Jesus around I need never be afraid. Amen.

HEROES

VALUE: Trust

BIBLE REFERENCES: Deuteronomy 31:8; Proverbs 3:25; John 11:1–44

TEACHING POINT: We can always trust God.

NOTES: Instructions are provided for the use of a sketch-board – the ladder letter words are underlined.

YOU WILL NEED: Prepared sketch-board and paints, PowerPoint or OHP acetate and pens (see introductory section on ladder lettering or visit **www.canicholls.com** and **www.childrensministry.co.uk** for information on how to purchase downloads).

Boys and girls, today I want to talk to you about heroes. Can anyone tell me what a hero is?

Let some of the children respond, and you can also ask them to name their favourite hero.

Yes – a hero is a person who comes along just at the right time when another person is in trouble and needs help. One day you may need a hero yourself. Or, you never know, one day *you* may be the hero. We often hear stories on the news about someone saving another person's life because they were there at the right time.

Well today I would like to tell you about <u>MY HERO</u>. My hero <u>JESUS</u>.

Draw cross.

Why is Jesus my hero? I will tell you in a minute, but before I do, I'd like to tell you a story from the Bible about three people who needed a hero. It will help you to understand why Jesus is my hero.

There were two sisters named Mary and Martha, and they were feeling <u>SAD</u>.

Draw in the two sad faces.

Their brother, Lazarus, was very ill. The family had all become good friends of Jesus and they knew that if they could get Jesus to come and see Lazarus, then everything would be OK. People felt really safe when Jesus was around. They didn't have hi-tech methods such as mobile phones or e-mail in those days to keep in touch, so they sent a messenger to go and find Jesus and tell him that his friend Lazarus was sick.

When Jesus heard about Lazarus, he told the messenger not to worry and said that everything was going to be all right. I expect Mary and Martha thought that Jesus would come running to see them straight away but, to everyone's surprise, he didn't. He left it a few days before he went to see Lazarus. Perhaps they thought, just like a lot of people think today, that Jesus had given up on them. Jesus had not given up on them for one minute, but he did want to prove a point. He wanted to prove to his friends that, as long as they trusted him, they never ever had to be afraid of death.

Eventually Jesus arrived in Bethany, the village where Mary, Martha and Lazarus lived. Jesus could see that everyone was crying and looking sad, and was told that Lazarus had already died and his body had been in a tomb for four days. So things were not only sad for Mary and Martha, but were now looking BAD. Really bad. Even Jesus got upset and cried when he saw how sad all the people were.

Martha said to Jesus, 'If only you had been here in time, my brother wouldn't have died!' Her family needed a hero. I expect they'd thought Jesus was that person, but now it all seemed too late. After all, Lazarus was dead.

One thing I have found with God is that he is never late and he is always there in times of trouble. In fact, the Bible teaches that God will never leave or forsake us. This is because God's heart is full of LOVE for people.

After Martha had finished speaking, Jesus said something really strange. He said, 'I am the resurrection and the life. He who believes in me will live, even though he dies; and whoever lives and believes in me will never die.' What Jesus was saying was that he had power over life and death, and all the time we put our trust in him we need never be afraid.

Then Jesus told them to roll away the big stone that covered the entrance of the tomb. Martha started to argue with Jesus, saying that the body would by now have started to decay, but Jesus just told them that all they had to do was trust him and everything would be OK.

Eventually the people did what they were told and rolled the stone away. First of all Jesus prayed, and then he shouted out to Lazarus and told him to come out of the tomb. Everyone was waiting to see what would happen. All of a sudden, Lazarus slowly walked out of the tomb! Everyone was amazed – Lazarus was alive!

Draw in happy face.

I expect they all ended up having a great big party.

So why is Jesus my hero? He is my hero because he can take all the sadness and all the badness out of any situation I may find myself in. Also, because of Jesus, I know that God loves and cares for me, and that he will never turn up too late. The Bible teaches that it is impossible for Jesus to be late because he is always there.

And because of Jesus I know that, even when I am no longer here on this earth, I will always have this: LIFE.

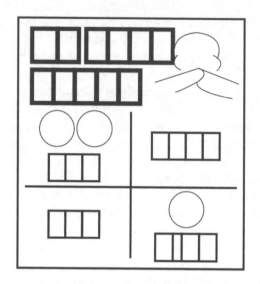

SUGGESTED SONGS:
Don't worry (37)
God knows the things we really need (59)
He's got the whole wide world (86)

SUGGESTED PRAYER:
Dear heavenly Father, whenever I am afraid, help me to know that I can always trust you to be there. Amen.

HOPE-ON-A-ROPE!

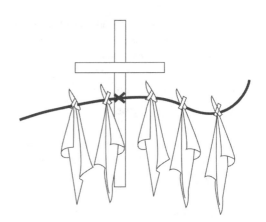

VALUES: Choosing right; Happiness; Honesty; Peace

BIBLE REFERENCE: 2 Corinthians 5:17

TEACHING POINT: Jesus can take all the bad and sad things away from our lives.

NOTES: This talk has been in my collection for many years. It uses one of those useful props that can make a very powerful object lesson. If you are unable to purchase it, it's simple to make, and you can use different coloured silks or hankies to highlight any specific thing you wish to draw attention to. Although I use silks for this object lesson, I always refer to them as 'hankies'. This enables the children to connect more easily, as they will all know what a hanky is.

YOU WILL NEED: One length of wood, 45 cm long x 2 cm square, designed so that part of the end pivots to form a cross; two pieces of rope, approximately 2 m in length; five silks (red, yellow, green, blue and white) hidden out of sight in a bag; one ordinary white hanky with a big black stain in the middle, also in the bag (see instructions at the end of this assembly).

Today, girls and boys, I am going to need three people to help me. Firstly, I will need two people to hold each end of these two ropes.

Pick two volunteers and give both of them one end of each rope. Ask them to move apart so the ropes are outstretched. Say to all the children that you need to find the middle of the ropes and perhaps they can help.

I need to find the middle of the ropes. If I run my finger along the ropes, can you say 'stop' when I get there?

They will shout 'stop' at the right place, but for fun I always overrun the spot, blaming the children for not being quick enough. Repeating this a couple of times creates some laughter and particularly suits my style – and possibly yours.

Eventually find the middle. Holding the piece of wood under the ropes at right angles, ask your helpers to drop the ends. Ask for a third volunteer to come and hold the piece of wood at the pivot end. Tie the ropes around the wood about a third of the way along from the other end. **(NB – Tying the ropes in the correct way is essential if this is to work properly – please see instructions.)** *After you have tied the ropes, hand the ends back to your first two helpers, whilst your third helper continues to hold the piece of wood. Have the bag with the hankies in it to hand. Now you are set for the rest of the talk.*

It doesn't matter what order you add the hankies to the ropes, but you should tie one corner of each hanky onto the ropes fairly loosely with a single knot, and end up with three hankies on one side of the cross and three on the other side.

Take out the red silk hanky.

As you can see, I have a red hanky. What does the colour red make you think of?

Allow some of the children to respond.

Red can remind us of danger. If you take the letter D off the front of the word 'danger', what word are you left with? Yes, you end up with the word 'anger'. How many of you have felt angry about something this week? It's quite natural to get angry sometimes but, if we're not careful, our anger can make us do some really silly things. If that happens, then we need to put back the D to make 'anger' spell 'danger'. Anger can be dangerous.

If possible, refer to people in the news or a personal situation.

I will tie the red hanky here to remind us that we have talked about anger and how it can lead to danger.

Tie the red silk hanky onto the rope. Take out the yellow one.

This time I have a yellow hanky. What does the colour yellow remind you of?

Allow some of the children to respond.

People might say someone is 'yellow' if they are scared of doing something. I have been scared lots of times in my life. Different people are scared of different things. Some people don't like the dark or spiders. Some people don't like being on the top of high buildings or flying in aeroplanes. Can you think of any other things people are scared of?

Allow some of the children to respond.

I will tie the yellow hanky onto the rope to remind us that we have talked about being scared.

Tie the yellow silk hanky onto the rope. Take out the green one.

Now, I have a green hanky. What does the colour green make you think of?

Allow some of the children to respond.

Has anyone heard the term 'green with envy'? Another word for envy is 'jealousy'. Have you ever been jealous of anyone?

Refer to the latest gadgets or games that some children may have, and explain how easy it is to get envious if we don't have the same.

If we are not careful, we can allow our jealousy to get the better of us and it can turn into anger – and what do we get if we put a D in front of anger? Yes, danger. Jealousy can cause people to do all sorts of nasty things like name-calling, bullying, fighting or lying. The Bible teaches that God does not want us to be like that towards other people. In fact, the Bible teaches that we should be the exact opposite, and love other people as much as we love ourselves.

I will tie the green hanky onto the rope to remind us that we have talked about being jealous.

Tie the green silk hanky onto the rope. Take out the blue one.

What about this blue hanky? What would it mean if I said I was 'feeling blue'?

Allow some of the children to respond.

We often refer to 'feeling blue' when we are sad. There is nothing wrong with feeling sad, even though we don't like that feeling. We all face difficult times in our lives when things happen to make us feel unhappy. Maybe you find it helpful to speak to a teacher or a friend if you are feeling sad about something. Since I've been a Christian, I have found that it is great to have a friend like Jesus – someone I can always turn to in times of trouble.

I will tie the blue hanky onto the rope to remind us that we have talked about being sad.

Tie the blue silk hanky onto the rope. Take out the white one.

Now then, what about the white hanky? What word do you think I will describe with this one? This might not be so easy, so I'll give you a clue. Sometimes I might tell a little white - - - what?

Allow some of the children to respond.

The word I am looking for is 'lie'. A 'white lie' means that I think I'm lying about something for a good reason. For example, if I am holding a surprise party for someone, I might tell that person I'm doing something different on that day, so as not to give the game away. However, if we tell a lie just so we can get our own way, or to blame someone else, that is a very selfish thing to do. It can also cause an innocent person to get into a lot of trouble. One of the things the Bible teaches is that we should always be truthful. A lot of people think that by telling lies they can get themselves out of trouble, when really it is the *truth* that sets you free.

I will tie the white hanky onto the rope to remind us that we have talked about telling lies.

Tie the white silk hanky onto the rope. Take out the ordinary white hanky with the stain in the centre.

This last hanky doesn't represent any particular word, but it represents our life in general and how all the things we have been talking about can mess it up. Our life starts out like this hanky did, all nice and clean. But it's not long before the bad things we do and say mess it all up. The Bible talks about those things being 'sin', and how sin is like a big stain that will not go away. Also, things can happen to us that make us frightened or sad, and those things can spoil our life too.

Tie the stained hanky onto the rope.

Many years ago, someone told me about Jesus. . .

Turn the top of the piece of wood into a cross.

. . .who died on the cross for all the bad things I have done. I prayed and asked Jesus to come and live in my heart and, when I did, something really strange and wonderful happened. Let me show you.

I found that I could give all my anger, fear, jealousy, sadness, lies and all the bad things I had ever done, to Jesus.

As you are saying this, you need to slide the hankies right into the centre of the rope, as close as possible to the cross on each side. Then take one of the ends of rope (it doesn't matter which one) from each child and swap them over, so that each child still has two ends to hold. **(This is really quite easy, but I would strongly advise you to practise it first. When you are in mid-flow of an assembly talk, it is very easy to miss this move, and if you do, the trick won't work and the object lesson fails!)** *Now assist the child holding the cross to pull the cross completely out of the tied ropes (making sure you are standing behind the child so as not to obscure the view), and ask the other two helpers to give a sharp little pull on the ropes. As they do so, all six hankies will just fall to the ground.*

You see, girls and boys, the Bible says that when we become a friend of Jesus, we become a new person. He will take away all the sad things and all the bad things in our life so that we really can live in the way that God always intended us to.

Pick up the hankies and refer to them one-by-one as you put them back into the bag.

Jesus helps me not to get angry *(red hanky),* not to be afraid *(yellow hanky)* and not to feel jealous *(green hanky).* He can turn my sadness into happiness *(blue hanky).* He helps me to be truthful *(white hanky).* And, most important of all *(stained hanky),* he takes away everything that stops me from being friends with God.

Thank the children for helping you, and get them to sit down to a round of applause from the other children.

SUGGESTED SONGS:
Be still (13)
Hands, hands, fingers, thumbs (76)
You shall go out with joy (249)

SUGGESTED PRAYER:
Dear Father, help me to place into your hands all my fears, worries and doubts. Please forgive me when I get angry or jealous. Help me to be pleased for others when they succeed, and help me to be the person you want me to be. Amen.

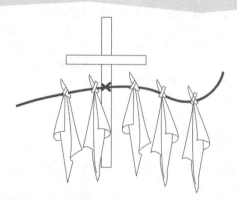

pdf available

Instructions for Hope on a Rope

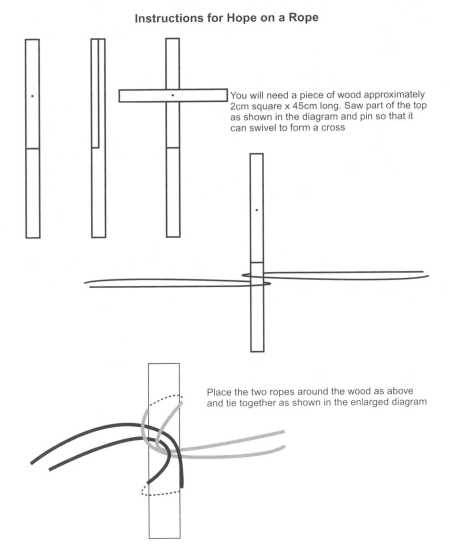

You will need a piece of wood approximately 2cm square x 45cm long. Saw part of the top as shown in the diagram and pin so that it can swivel to form a cross

Place the two ropes around the wood as above and tie together as shown in the enlarged diagram

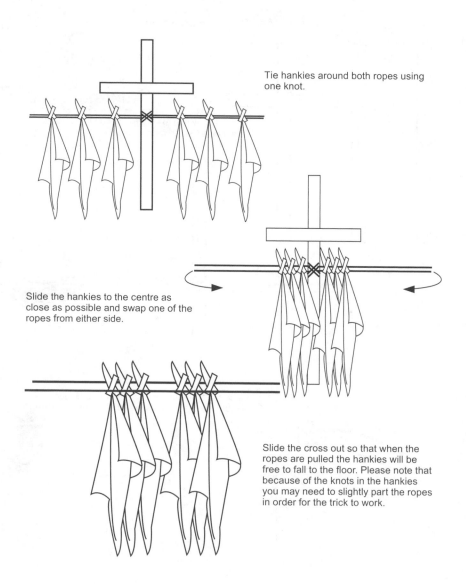

Tie hankies around both ropes using one knot.

Slide the hankies to the centre as close as possible and swap one of the ropes from either side.

Slide the cross out so that when the ropes are pulled the hankies will be free to fall to the floor. Please note that because of the knots in the hankies you may need to slightly part the ropes in order for the trick to work.

pdf available

IF THE HAT FITS...

VALUES: Co-operation; Self-worth

BIBLE REFERENCE: Ephesians 2:10

TEACHING POINT: Everyone is different but necessary to each other and equally important to God.

NOTES: This is a really fun assembly to do. It is very interactive and easily adjusted depending on the age of the children. The characters you choose are really up to you, and you will need as many characters as you have letters in your chosen word (see below), but these are the ones I have found to work well:

- Fireman (helmet)
- Actor (cowboy hat)

- Scientist (oversized glasses)
- Sailor (cap)
- Pop star ('Elvis' wig)
- Granny (old lady's hat)
- Swimmer (hat)
- Policeman (helmet)
- Teacher (mortar-board)

YOU WILL NEED: Placards, each with a big, bold letter so that your chosen word (*FRIEND, NEIGHBOUR or COMMUNITY*) can be spelt out; hats or other props to suit the characters you decide to use – all of which can be purchased from your local party costume shop.

You will need as many volunteers as you have letter placards. Ask for a volunteer. For example:

Who would like to be a policeman or a policewoman when they leave school? That's a really important job. We need to have policemen and women, don't we?

Ask each volunteer to come up separately and give him/her the relevant prop. As the child puts on the prop (with laughter from the other children), explain the importance of the job they are doing. For the scientist I always choose a small child and give them the oversized glasses to wear. This works really well if you stand in front of the child with your back to the audience as you fit the glasses. The laughter is immense when you suddenly reveal this small person wearing a huge pair of glasses!

Once each child is wearing their prop, get them to stand in a row and give them a letter in the pre-determined jumbled order below (i.e. they will form an anagram).

These letters spell a word, but they are in the wrong order. I'll give you some clues as to what the word is.

<u>For infants or juniors</u>: **REDFIN (FRIEND)** *(6 letters)* *(Clues:* R = Ready to help you; E = Everyone needs them; D = Do things together; F = Fun to be with; I = Important to you; N = Nice to each other.)*

For juniors: **ROUGHBINE (NEIGHBOUR)** *(9 letters)* *(Clues:* R = Reliable; O = On hand if you need something; U = Understanding; G = Go out of their way to help you; H = Happy to see you; B = By your side in times of trouble; I = Interested in you; N = Nice to be with; E = Easy to get along with.)

Alternative: **TUMMYCOIN (COMMUNITY)** *(9 letters)* *(Clues:* T = Trustworthy; U = Understanding; M = Manners; M = Mild-tempered; Y = Yes-people (i.e. positive, helpful attitude); C = Concerned for each other; O = On hand if you need something; I = Interested in other people; N = Nice to be with.)

When they have guessed what the word is, ask the children holding the letters to sort themselves out (keeping hold of their letter) so that they spell the word correctly. Encourage the older children to help the younger ones.

At this point, turn to the main assembly and say:

Do you see how everyone is having to work together in order to spell the word correctly? When we all work together, it does make life much easier.

When everyone is in their right place, explain:

Every letter is equally important. If you take one away, the word doesn't make sense any more.

Illustrate this by getting one of the children in the middle to turn round, having the effect of taking that letter away.

We need police officers to keep order. We need granny to look after us if our parents have to go out and don't want us to be left alone, and so on. All of us need each other.

Now, you may think the last letter in the word is the least important, because it comes at the end. But if you take it away. . .

Get the last child to turn round.

. . .the word still loses its meaning. So, you see, even the last letter is just as important as the rest.

You may think that you are not as important as some other people in your class because they might be good at something that you're not so good at, like sums or spelling. Maybe you don't have as many things as some of your friends. Or perhaps you've got into trouble. Or perhaps you feel lonely, or worried about the future, or that nobody cares about you.

But you are just as important as everyone else. If you weren't in this school, this school just wouldn't be the same – because there is only one of you. You are unique and special, and you cannot be replaced.

The Bible teaches that everybody, including you, is important to Jesus – whatever anyone else thinks about you, and whatever you think about yourself.

If somebody were to die for you, you would probably think that you must have been very special to that person. The Bible teaches, and Christians believe, that is exactly what Jesus did for us. When Jesus was crucified – which means that he died on a cross – the Bible teaches that he died for us all because he loves us very much, and that he rose again from the dead and is alive today. The Bible goes on to tell us that if we say 'sorry' to God for the wrong things we have done, and ask Jesus to be our friend – he will. When we become friends with Jesus, we also become friends with God – and that's pretty special.

Ask the children to hand back their props, and have them sit down to a round of applause for being great helpers.

SUGGESTED SONGS:
Father God created the world (42)
God gave me ears (55)
Jesus put this song into our hearts (129)

SUGGESTED PRAYER:
Dear Father, help me to understand that I am not only special, but also important. Help me to use the special gifts and abilities that you have given me in a way that helps others. Amen.

JACK THE LAD

VALUE: Saying sorry

BIBLE REFERENCE: Luke 15:11–32

TEACHING POINT: God wants to forgive us if we say sorry when we do wrong.

NOTES: This talk deliberately uses simple key words to make it accessible to younger children. Instructions are provided for the use of a sketch-board – the ladder letter words are underlined.

YOU WILL NEED: Prepared sketch-board and paints, PowerPoint or OHP acetate and pens (see introductory section on ladder lettering or visit **www.canicholls.com** and **www.childrensministry.co.uk** for information on how to purchase downloads).

Jesus told a story about a young man who thought he was ever so important. Jesus didn't give him a name – so let's call him JACK THE LAD!

Jack the Lad lived in a lovely home, all warm and cosy, and there was a hot dinner waiting for him every day. But was he satisfied? Oh no! In fact, he was fed up. . .

Draw in angry face.

. . .and he thought, 'Here I am, day in, day out, stuck at home, just helping out around the place, being made use of. I'm not important here. I want to be noticed! I want to do my own thing! It's my right!' And he worked himself up into a tizzy and got angry and MAD.

He said to his dad, 'Dad, you know all that money you're going to leave me in your will when you die?' His dad said, 'Y-e-s. . .' Jack said, 'Well, can I have it now? Then I can leave home and have some fun.'

Surprisingly, his dad said 'yes'. He gave Jack the money and watched him disappear into the distance and go his own way. When *we* decide to go our own way, like Jack, the Bible teaches that God doesn't stop us. He never forces us to do what we don't want to do.

Well, Jack the Lad went far away to another country. He thought, 'At last, I'm free! I can do whatever I want!' And because he had lots of money, he had lots of friends. They had wild parties every night. . .

Draw in manic face.

. . .there was lots of dancing, lots of eating, and lots of throwing up afterwards! And Jack got up to all kinds of mischief. In fact, the life he was leading was very, very BAD.

But then – guess what? Jack's money ran out. So all his friends ran out too! At the same time, there was a famine in that country, which meant that even the food ran out. The only job Jack could get was looking after pigs. He was so hungry that even the scraps he was feeding to the pigs looked good.

Poor Jack sat in the pigsty. . .

Draw in miserable face.

. . .and he realised he'd made a big mistake. He wished he hadn't left his lovely home and wasted his dad's money. Jack the Lad felt so SAD. And he didn't feel important any more – he felt very, very small.

Then Jack remembered all the good things about his home – especially the food! He got up and started on the long walk back. As he trudged along. . .

Draw in worried face with thought bubbles.

. . .he thought about what he would say when he got home. Something like, '<u>DAD</u>, I'm sorry. Please forgive me. Can I come back home – not as your son but just as your servant?!' And he was worried – 'What on earth is Dad going to say? He's bound to be angry. Oh dear!'

What Jack didn't realise was that, all this time, his dad had been looking out for him. And as soon as he saw Jack in the distance, he ran to meet him and flung his arms around him – even though Jack was filthy and sweaty and hadn't had a bath for weeks!

When we realise that we've been turning our back on God and disobeying him and doing our own thing, the Bible says that we only have to turn back to God and he'll come running to meet us. And he won't be angry with us either.

Well, Dad forgave Jack straight away. . .

Draw in happy face.

. . .and told the servants to clean him up and dress him in smart clothes and prepare a feast to celebrate. Jack the Lad felt extremely <u>GLAD</u>. He knew he was important to his dad after all.

But then Jack's older brother, Fred, started moaning and whingeing, 'It's not fair! I've been here all the time, working my fingers to the bone. Surely I'm more important than this silly little boy? But you've never had a feast for me.'

Dad said to Fred, 'Of course you're important, Fred. All I have is yours. But your brother Jack is important too, and so we have to celebrate because he's come back home.'

Of course we're all different from each other. But although we're all different, the Bible says we're all equally important to God. No one is more important than anyone else, and no one is less important than anyone else. And if you want to know just how important and special we all are to God. . .

Draw in the cross.

. . .remember that the Bible teaches that Jesus died on the cross to take the punishment for all our selfishness *(point to MAD),* and sin *(point to BAD),* so that if we're really sorry *(point to SAD)* and tell God we want to change *(point to DAD),* then God will forgive us and we can live with him for ever in heaven *(point to GLAD).*

I'm really glad about that, aren't you?

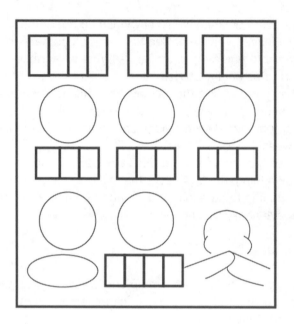

JOSEPH IS A WORRIED MAN

I'm Worried

VALUES: Hope; Trust

BIBLE REFERENCE: Matthew 1:18–25; Matthew 2:1–2; Luke 1:26–38, 2:1–20

TEACHING POINT: God has a plan for each of us.

NOTES: This is what I call an instant play. The children love being involved and there is no rehearsal. You will need to use your imagination for the costumes, which can be made from old bits of sheeting, tea towels, etc. These need to be made so that they just wrap around the children or slip on and off quickly. Keep the whole thing simple – the simpler the better.

YOU WILL NEED: Costumes for: Joseph, Mary, Inn-keeper, Shepherd, Wise Man, King Herod; one large pair of comical spectacles; one crown; a black face-painting crayon; seven large cards, each containing one of the following phrases: 'I'm Worried', 'I'm Mean', 'I'm Excited', 'I'm Grumpy', 'I'm Clever', 'I'm Happy', 'I'm Exhausted!'

Today, girls and boys, I thought we would do a play, and so I will need some volunteers to help. Who is going to be the first?

Pick a child, ask him to put on the tea-towel, etc., and paint on a little moustache. This always gets a laugh if you stand in front of the child so the other children can't see what you have done until the last minute. Then give the child the 'I'm Worried' card to hold.

Girls and boys, I would like to introduce you to Mr Joseph. Now, Mr Joseph is a worried man because his wife is going to have a baby. You don't realise the worry we men go through when our wives are having babies! It's all right for our wives because they have all the comfort of being looked after, but we men are just left to do all the worrying.

(Please note that this is obviously said tongue-in-cheek but only works if a man is telling the story with adults present.)

Well, Joseph was worried, not only because his wife Mary was expecting a baby, but also because they had to go on a long journey to a place called Bethlehem to register their names.

Right, now we need someone to be Mary. Who wants to be Mary?

Pick a child and ask her to put on the costume.

So, off down the dusty road went Joseph and Mary. They had to travel about 70 miles, but they didn't have cars or skateboards in those days. They only had a donkey, and so it would have taken them a long time.

Eventually they reached Bethlehem, and now they needed to find somewhere to stay because it was nearly time for Mary to give birth.

We need another person to help.

Pick a child and ask him/her to dress up in the inn-keeper's clothes and give him/her the 'I'm Mean' card to hold.

Joseph was trying to find a place for Mary to give birth to the baby Jesus, but there was no one willing to help out. Joseph knocked on the doors of the inns, but as soon as the inn-keepers saw Mary and the condition she was in, they said, 'Go away!' Just like today sometimes people can be ever so mean. If there is nothing in it for them, they just don't want to know. You're not like that, are you?

Eventually one of the inn-keepers said there was a stable round the back and they could use that.

Now we need a person to represent the shepherds. Who would like to do that?

Pick a child and ask him/her to dress up in the shepherd's clothes and give him/her the 'I'm Excited' card to hold.

That night, when Jesus was born, there were some shepherds in a field, looking after their sheep. All of a sudden, the sky was ablaze with angels! One angel told the shepherds about Jesus being born in a stable. They were so excited to hear about Jesus that they ran as fast as they could to look for him. They didn't think about their sheep. They just left everything to go and search for Jesus.

Today, girls and boys, some people are happy and excited to hear about Jesus. They will do anything to learn about him. But some people are like my next character.

We need another person to help. We need someone to play the part of King Herod. Who would like to do that?

Pick a child and give him a crown to wear and the 'I'm Grumpy' card to hold.

When Jesus was born, there were some mean people, there were some excited people, and there were some grumpy people as well. When King Herod heard that a child had been born, and it was said that this child was going to grow up and be king, oh boy, did he get grumpy! He shouted, 'King? *I'm* the King! No one is going to rule over me! Who is this Jesus anyway?'

It's still the same even today when you talk to people about Jesus. Some people get very excited – just like the shepherds. And some people get grumpy – just like King Herod. They don't want anyone ruling over their lives. Are you like that – the king of your patch, and no one is going to tell you what to do?

Well, King Herod was so grumpy about Jesus that he made plans to have him killed. I wonder what happened next?

Who is going to help me now? We need a person to represent the wise men.

Pick a child and give him the large spectacles to wear and the 'I'm Clever' card to hold.

There were wise men from the east who had heard about Jesus and followed a star in the sky that they believed would lead them to where Jesus was. On the way they met up with King Herod, who pretended that he was interested in meeting Jesus. He told them to let him know when they had found the baby. But they were wise and clever. They discovered that King Herod really wanted Jesus out of the way, and so they decided not to tell. When they found out where Jesus was, they took him some gifts and then said goodbye, and went back to their homes by another route to avoid seeing King Herod again.

While all this was going on, poor Mr Joseph was getting more and more worried. There was really no need for Joseph to be worried, because all the time God was looking after him and his family. One night an angel warned Joseph in a dream about King Herod, and told him to take Mary and Jesus far away to Egypt and wait until he was told it was safe to return.

Even though Joseph didn't realise it at the time, it was all working out as God had planned it. The Bible teaches that God has a plan for each and every one of us. All we need to do is trust him.

(You can elaborate here if you wish and refer to the gospel message.)

In the end it all worked out OK for Mr Joseph, and he ended up like this.

Exchange Joseph's card for the one with the words: 'I'm Happy'.

But what about Mary? We shouldn't forget Mary, should we? I wonder how she is feeling in all of this.

Give Mary the 'I'm Exhausted!' card to hold. This ending is unexpected and will normally get a laugh, especially from the adults. (For things to be funny, the timing needs to be right. Don't be afraid of getting it wrong, though – you will learn from your mistakes!)

SUGGESTED SONGS:
Child in a manger born (22)
He's got the whole wide world (86)

SUGGESTED PRAYER:
Dear Father in heaven, just as you had a plan for Jesus, you also have a plan for my life. Help me always to put my trust in you and to know that your plans never go wrong. Amen.

LEARN OR BURN?

VALUES: Forgiveness; Humility

BIBLE REFERENCES: Genesis 37, 39, 41 – 45

TEACHING POINT: God can help us learn from all the bad things that happen to us.

NOTES: Instructions are provided for the use of a sketch-board – the ladder letter words are underlined.

YOU WILL NEED: Prepared sketch-board and paints, PowerPoint or OHP acetate and pens (see introductory section on ladder lettering or visit **www.canicholls.com** and **www.childrensministry.co.uk** for information on how to purchase downloads).

Have you ever had someone, or some people, do something nasty to you? When that happens, how do you react? Do you <u>BURN</u> with anger? <u>OR</u> do you <u>LEARN</u> from the experience?

It's quite natural to get angry when people treat you in a bad way, but you do have two choices. One is to *learn* from that situation and become a better person, and the other is to *burn* with anger and become a bitter person. There are many people walking around today full of anger and bitterness, and the only people they are hurting are themselves.

I want to tell you a story about a man from the Bible who lived many years before Jesus. His name was Joseph. Joseph had a special gift, a special ability. He was able to tell people the meaning of their dreams. One night Joseph himself had a strange dream. In this dream God showed Joseph that he was going to be really important – so important that his own family would bow down before him. Joseph told his family about his dream, and his brothers became jealous of him. They were so jealous that they wanted to get rid of him. They *burned* with anger.

Ask the children if they have ever been jealous, or ask them to give some examples of what it means to be jealous.

Jealousy is a terrible thing, and if we allow it to get hold of us, we can end up doing all sorts of silly things.

Joseph's brothers did just that. And all of a sudden, Joseph found himself in this situation.

Draw heads peering into the well.

His brothers threw him down a well, a big hole in the ground. This was a real <u>BLOW</u> for Joseph. One minute he is told by God that he is going to be important, and the next minute he is in a hole in the ground, surrounded by people who hate him. Things were looking pretty grim for Joseph now.

Life sometimes suddenly gets difficult and deals you a blow, doesn't it, girls and boys? When this happens, how do you respond? Do you *learn*? Or do you *burn*?

Now, Joseph probably thought that things couldn't get much worse. But do you know what? They did!

Draw chain between ball and manacle.

His brothers saw some slave traders and decided to get rid of Joseph that way. They also thought they could make some money into the bargain. So they pulled Joseph out of the well and sold him to the slave traders. Poor Joseph! How do you think he must have felt? Would he *learn*? Or would he *burn*? He had done nothing wrong, and yet overnight he had gone from feeling that he was someone special, to feeling absolutely <u>LOW</u>.

Talk a little about slaves, and the fact that slaves had no rights and their lives were worth nothing.

Joseph was taken by the slave traders all the way to Egypt and sold again to a man named Potiphar.

Draw man in window.

Potiphar was one of the king's officers. He had plenty of money and a large house. He needed someone to be in charge of his house when he was away, and he could see there was something special about Joseph. He could see that Joseph was a person who could be trusted and so he thought that Joseph was the man for the job. Joseph started to feel better about his situation. Things were beginning to look up.

Isn't it funny though, girls and boys, how life can be OK one minute, and then something comes along and knocks you down? That's just how it was for Joseph. There was Joseph, getting on with his job, minding his own business, when along comes Mrs Potiphar. Now, she was not a very nice person. One day when Mr Potiphar was away on business, she said to Joseph, 'Give us a kiss!' She fancied Joseph, but Joseph loved God and knew it would not be right to kiss another man's wife, and so he refused. Mrs Potiphar didn't like being rejected, and she was so angry that when Mr Potiphar got home, she told lies about Joseph. She said that Joseph had attacked her. Poor Joseph ended up like this.

Draw prison bars.

Joseph was thrown into prison. How do think he felt now? Would he *learn* from his situation? Or would he *burn*? Many people would think 'I want to <u>FIGHT</u>'. Many people would be burning with anger by now, and would want to fight the world. Joseph had been thrown down a well, sold as a slave, and now thrown into prison for something he hadn't done. He's done everything right as far as God is concerned, and what thanks does he get? You would think that if anyone had the right to get angry and fight, it would be Joseph. But do you know what? He didn't. I think that deep down in his heart he trusted that God would eventually sort things out. He kept his nose clean and just made the best of a bad situation.

It wasn't long before the prison governor could see that Joseph could be trusted, and so Joseph was – again – given important jobs to do like looking after the other prisoners. The Bible actually says that even though Joseph was in prison, God was with him and looking after him. In fact, God had a very special job for Joseph, as we shall find out.

Two years later, the king of Egypt had a dream and was troubled by it. He called all his top advisers to see if they could tell him what the dream meant, but nobody could. Then someone remembered Joseph in prison. They said to the king, 'I think there's a chap in prison who can tell the meaning of dreams.' 'Bring him here at once!' shouted the king.

Joseph was brought to see the king, and the king told Joseph about his dream. Joseph told the king that his dream meant there was going to be a famine. That means there would be no food because there was going to be no rain and so the crops wouldn't grow. Joseph said that the dream meant that first there would be seven years of plenty, but after that there would be seven years of nothing. Joseph advised the king to store up enough food during the first seven years of plenty to make sure there would be enough food to last during the famine.

The king was so impressed with Joseph that he put him in charge of the whole country! He knew Joseph could be trusted and that he would do a good job.

Anyway, seven years later when the famine started, and the neighbouring lands ran out of food, who should come knocking on the door? Yes, it was *Joseph's brothers*, who were desperate for some food. They didn't recognise Joseph. It had been many years since they had seen him. He was now all grown up and spoke in a different language. Joseph knew that they were his brothers, but he didn't let on. What should he do? Joseph could now get his own back if he wanted to, because he actually had the power to have his brothers executed!

But Joseph was not a person to *burn* with anger. Joseph used difficult situations to *learn* and better himself. As we can see, it definitely paid off in the long run. In fact, Joseph became one of Israel's greatest people, but it did take thirteen years of hard struggle.

Joseph couldn't hold back any longer, and had to tell his brothers who he was, and eventually the whole family were reunited. Joseph decided it was far better to forgive his brothers. Sometimes it can be really difficult to forgive people, but the Bible teaches that we must. One of the things we learn from Jesus is the importance of forgiving others when they do wrong things to us.

Draw in cross.

When Jesus was nailed to a cross, the Bible teaches that he had done nothing wrong. In fact, he was taking the blame for all the naughty things we do that make God sad. As Jesus was dying on the cross, he called out, 'Father, forgive them because they don't know what they are doing.'

I have learnt many things by following Jesus, and I think Joseph knew this as well. When we use a bad situation to *learn*, and don't allow ourselves to *burn*, we can be <u>FREE</u>. And when you are free on the inside, then you really are free.

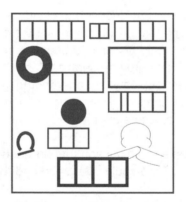

SUGGESTED SONGS:
For if you forgive (47)
Jubilate, everybody (135)

SUGGESTED PRAYER:
Dear Father in heaven, when things go wrong and other people hurt me, please help me not to burn with anger and seek revenge, but to learn from every situation whether it be good or bad. Forgive me for the times I have hurt other people, and help me to forgive others when they hurt me. Help me to be more like Jesus every day. Amen.

MONSTERS

N	M	R	A	P	P	E	R
A	O	F	R	C	A	N	R
P	R	T	H	E	P	E	T
B	F	S	H	R	D	V	C
S	A	R	B	I	I	R	A
F	X	G	R	R	N	C	R
T	L	O	V	E	A	G	P
J	R	D	R	I	P	R	U
E	T	A	R	A	P	E	S

Romans 8:39
NOTHING CAN SEPARATE US FROM THE LOVE OF GOD

VALUES: Love; Tolerance

BIBLE REFERENCE: Romans 8:38–39

TEACHING POINT: Nothing can separate us from the love of God.

NOTES: This assembly starts with a memory verse word-search using Romans 8:39: 'Nothing can separate us from the love of God.' Hide the words from this scripture among other letters in a grid, making it into a word-search. Have the verse spelt out across the top or bottom. Then tell the children that you'd like them to come up one by one and highlight the hidden words. When this has been completed, you can use the puppet routine below to reinforce the scripture verse.

YOU WILL NEED: Puppet, prepared word-search on sketch-board or OHP acetate (visit **www.canicholls.com** and **www.childrensministry.co.uk** for information on how to purchase downloads).

Start with the memory verse word-search. Read out the verse and repeat it all together. Then introduce your puppet.

YOU	You were making a lot of noise last night.
PUPPET	Yes, there is something ugly in the case.
YOU	What – like a monster?
PUPPET	Yes, and it's ugly.
YOU	There are really no such things as monsters. I'm sure there is a simple explanation.
PUPPET	No – it's ugly! Don't look!
YOU	*(Go into the case and pull out a mirror.)* Is this what you were looking at?
PUPPET	*(Show the puppet the mirror. As you do, the puppet makes a noise to indicate that he's frightened.)* Take it away – it's ugly! It's ugly!
YOU	Look, it's a mirror. It's your own reflection!
PUPPET	*(Looks gingerly into the mirror.)* Is that me in there?
YOU	Yes, it's you.
PUPPET	Oh, nice!
YOU	You see, I told you there were no such things as monsters.
PUPPET	Look at all the girls and boys – they're ugly!
YOU	No they are not, and they're not monsters.
PUPPET	Yes they are. One called me a name.
YOU	Oh really? What did they call you?
PUPPET	Wooden-head!
YOU	And what did you say?
PUPPET	Fish-face!
YOU	God doesn't like it when we call one another names.
PUPPET	Does God stop liking us?
YOU	No, God will never stop liking us. The Bible teaches that nothing can separate us from the love of God.
PUPPET	Even when we're naughty?
YOU	Yes, even when we're naughty. He doesn't like girls and boys doing naughty things, but the Bible teaches that nothing can separate us from the love of God.
PUPPET	What about when they say naughty words?
YOU	God loves all the girls and boys, even the ones who say naughty

words. He doesn't like them to say naughty words, but the Bible teaches that nothing can separate us from the love of God.

PUPPET   What about when they fight in the playground?

YOU   Well, again, God doesn't want girls and boys to fight. But he still loves those boys and girls, because the Bible teaches. . . *(look at the children)* . . .What does the Bible teach, girls and boys?

Get the children to repeat the memory verse. Get the puppet to say 'cheerio', and put him back in the case.

SUGGESTED SONGS:
Come on and celebrate (26)
God loves you and I love you (61)

SUGGESTED PRAYER:
Dear Father, please forgive us when we doubt and lose faith and stop trusting in you. Help us to know and understand that you are always there and that nothing can separate us from your love. Amen.

MR GRABBIT

VALUES: Generosity; Happiness

BIBLE REFERENCE: Matthew 6:19–21

TEACHING POINT: Know the joy of giving

NOTES: Instructions are provided for the use of a sketch-board – the ladder letter words are underlined.

YOU WILL NEED: Prepared sketch-board and paints, PowerPoint or OHP acetate and pens (see introductory section on ladder lettering or visit **www.canicholls.com** and **www.childrensministry.co.uk** for information on how to purchase downloads).

Today I want to tell you the story of <u>MR GRABBIT</u>. Mr Grabbit loved money. He grabbed as much as he could. And he spent it all on himself. He was very, very selfish.

Mr Grabbit bought himself. . .

Draw house.

. . .a house. But this was no ordinary house. It was the biggest house you've ever seen. It had an indoor heated swimming pool, and gold taps in all the bathrooms. Mr Grabbit loved his house. It made him feel important. But he wasn't really happy. He was always <u>BOTHERED</u> that it might get *burgled*.

Then Mr Grabbit bought himself. . .

Draw jet.

. . .a private jet. But this was no ordinary jet. It was the fastest, most modern aeroplane you've ever seen. He would even fly over to Paris for lunch. Mr Grabbit loved his jet. It made him feel important. But he wasn't really happy. He was always <u>CONCERNED</u> that it might *crash*.

Then Mr Grabbit bought himself. . .

Draw yacht.

. . .a yacht. But this was no ordinary yacht. It was the most luxurious yacht you've ever seen. Mr Grabbit loved his yacht. It made him feel important. But he wasn't really happy. He was always <u>SCARED</u> that it might *sink*.

Mr Grabbit thought to himself, 'I'm a success. I've got everything money can buy. But I'm not really happy. What shall I do? I know – I'll grab even more things for myself!'

But then Mr Grabbit had a *really worrying* thought. 'When I die,' he thought, 'I won't be able to take any of my possessions with me!' And that thought plunged him into <u>MISERY</u>.

Then, one day, Mr Grabbit happened to be staying in an extremely posh hotel. And on his extremely posh bedside table there happened to be a Bible. Mr Grabbit opened the Bible at any old page, and do you know what he read? He read, 'Do not store up for yourselves treasures on earth, where moth and rust destroy, and thieves break in and steal. But store up for yourselves treasures in heaven.'

Mr Grabbit hadn't got the faintest idea how he could store up treasures in heaven. So he carried on reading the Bible to try and find out. And he learnt that God didn't want him to be a grabbing sort of person – God wanted him to be a *giving* sort of person. *That* is the way he could store up treasures in heaven!

The Bible tells us that God himself is a giving sort of person, because 2,000 years ago he sent his only Son, Jesus, into the world. . .

Draw cross.

. . .to die on a cross so that all the wrong things we've ever done can be forgiven by God, as long as we ask him to forgive us – and then we can live with him for ever in heaven.

Well, Mr Grabbit thought, 'I don't really need a luxury yacht.' So. . .

Cross out yacht.

. . .he sold his yacht and gave the money to the poor. And he felt <u>SATISFIED</u>. Then he thought, 'I don't really need a private jet.' So. . .

Cross out jet.

. . .he sold his jet and gave the money to the poor. And he felt <u>CONTENT</u>. Then he thought, 'I don't really need an enormous house.' So. . .

Cross out house.

. . .he sold his house and gave the money to the poor. And he felt all happy and <u>BOUNCY</u>.

And then Mr Grabbit had a *really wonderful* thought. 'I haven't even died yet,' he thought, 'but I've already found real treasure, and it's got absolutely nothing to do with possessions!'

And the name of that treasure is <u>JOY</u>.

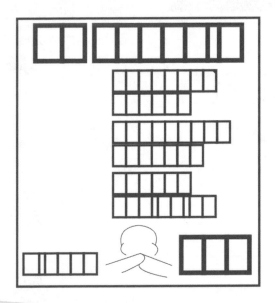

SUGGESTED SONGS:
Do not store up (33)
One in a million (168)
Store up yourself some treasure (190)

SUGGESTED PRAYER:
Dear Father, help me not to be greedy and to understand the joy of giving. Also, help me to be grateful for the things that I have and know that real contentment, satisfaction and joy come from knowing you. Amen.

NEW LIFE IN JESUS

VALUE: Freedom

BIBLE REFERENCES: Matthew 27:11–26; Mark 15:1–15; Luke 23:1–25; John 18:28–40

TEACHING POINT: Jesus died for me.

NOTES: This assembly is an ideal talk for Easter, although it can be used at any time. Instructions are provided for the use of a sketch-board – the ladder letter words are underlined.

YOU WILL NEED: Cut out some card so that when it is folded it will form a small box or cube about 10 cm square and when the cube is opened, it will form a cross. Write GOD'S SON on the squares (see picture above). Prepared sketch-board and paints, PowerPoint or OHP acetate and pens (see introductory section on ladder lettering or visit **www.canicholls.com** and **www.childrensministry.co.uk** for information on how to purchase downloads).

Start by holding up the box.

This is my best gift and it always reminds me of Easter. Would you like to see what it is? Well, I will show you in a minute, but first I want to ask you a question. What do you like best about Easter?

Let some of the children respond, and pick up on the ones who say Easter eggs.

Yes, we love Easter eggs, don't we? But can anyone tell me why we have Easter eggs at Easter?

Let two or three have a guess.

Well, I will tell you. The reason we have Easter eggs is because it makes us think of life – <u>NEW LIFE</u>. Now, here is someone who has got life, but it isn't new life.

Draw in the down strokes of the prison bars.

Can you tell me what is happening here? Yes, it's someone in prison. Do you think this person is happy in prison? No! What do you think would make that person happy? Yes, freedom.

Draw in the legs of the person to make it look as though they are now on the outside of the prison.

Do you know, children, there are a lot of people walking around today who are free on the outside, but they are not free on the inside. This is because we can be imprisoned by whatever it is that controls us. Some people are controlled by fear, and some people are unable to control their temper – it controls them. (*Give other examples that you may feel appropriate.*)
The Bible teaches that God doesn't want us to be controlled by anger, worry or fear, but that God wants us to be controlled by his Spirit. Only then can we be truly <u>FREE</u>.

Draw in a smiley face.

Now, many years ago, there was a man in prison in a place called Jerusalem. His name was Barabbas. He had been very bad. He was full of <u>ANGER</u>.

Draw an angry-looking face.

(You can also, depending on time, pick up on the silly things we can do when we are angry that can get us into trouble, and say that some people even end up like Barabbas.)

In fact, Barabbas had been so bad that the authorities decided he should be put to death.

Well, he woke up on the day of his execution feeling very scared. He didn't want to die. He could hear the jailer outside jangling his keys. As the key turned in the lock, Barabbas's teeth started to chatter and his knees started to knock together. When the jailer walked in, Barabbas shouted, 'I'm sorry, I didn't mean to do it, it was an accident, I want my mum!' The jailer said to Barabbas, 'OK, you can go!' 'What?!' said Barabbas. 'OK, you can go!' the jailer repeated. 'If you don't hurry up, I will change my mind.' Barabbas ran out of that jail as fast as his legs would carry him.

When Barabbas got outside, there was a lot of commotion going on and he could see a man. . .

Draw in the cross.

. . .carrying a cross. Barabbas went up to someone and asked, 'What's going on?' 'Oh, they're going to nail someone to a cross.' 'What's his name, what has he done?' Barabbas asked. 'I think it's someone called Jesus, and I don't think he's actually done anything wrong,' the man replied. 'All I know is, there was a big meeting in town and this man, Jesus, was on trial, but they couldn't find anything wrong in him. In fact, he has only ever done good things. The governor was going to let him go, but all the people, for some reason, shouted, "No, let Barabbas go free instead, and kill Jesus!" ' 'Well, I'm Barabbas!' said Barabbas. 'In that case, Jesus is taking your place. He is dying for you!'

In fact, children, the Bible teaches, and Christians believe, that Jesus didn't just die for Barabbas. . .

At this point, open the box to show the cross with the words GOD'S SON.

. . .but that he died for us all. It says that 'God so loved the world that he gave his only Son that anyone who believes in him should not perish, but have eternal life.'

Let me explain what this means. The Bible teaches that, just like the law courts have to punish some people and send them to prison, God has to punish sin – that is, all our bad words, all our bad thoughts, and all the bad things we do. The thing is that God loves us so much that he really doesn't want to punish us, and that is why he sent Jesus to take our place.

All we have to do is say 'sorry' to God and ask Jesus to be our friend, and then we are free! And when we have Jesus as our friend, he helps us not to be controlled by anger or worry or fear, and so we really can be free. We can have a new life <u>IN JESUS</u>.

SUGGESTED SONGS:
Easter jubilation (40)
Lord, I lift your name on high (143)

SUGGESTED PRAYER:
Dear Father in heaven, thank you for sending Jesus to die for me. Thank you, also, that because of Jesus I can now be your friend. Help me to be free from anything that stops me living the life you intended for me. Amen.

RESCUED!

VALUE: Obedience

BIBLE REFERENCE: Jonah 1 – 4; Psalm 18:6

TEACHING POINT: We should try and do what God wants us to.

NOTES: Instructions are provided for the use of a sketch-board – the ladder letter words are underlined.

YOU WILL NEED: Prepared sketch-board and paints, PowerPoint or OHP acetate and pens (see introductory section on ladder lettering or visit **www.canicholls.com** and **www.childrensministry.co.uk** for information on how to purchase downloads).

Hands up if you like eating fish. Now, hands up if you would like to be *eaten by a fish!* What a terrible thought!

There's someone in the Old Testament of the Bible who was swallowed up by an extremely big fish – but he lived to tell the tale, because he was <u>RESCUED.</u>

His name was Jonah, and he was a Jew. At that time, the very worst enemies of the Jews were the Assyrians. The Assyrians used to do some violent and cruel things. And when Jonah thought about them, he felt <u>HATE</u>.

Have you ever hated someone who's been nasty – either to you or to someone else? It's a natural reaction. But that doesn't mean it's the right reaction. When you hate someone, it makes you feel all churned up inside. It can even make you ill. Some people go all through their lives hating someone – and it ruins their lives.

God didn't hate the Assyrians. Surprisingly, he felt <u>LOVE</u> for them. What he did hate was their bad behaviour. There's a difference. Their bad behaviour made him sad, and he wanted them to change – because he loved them.

So one day God said to Jonah, 'I want you to get on a ship and go to Nineveh – which was the main city of the Assyrians – and warn the people that if they carry on in this terrible way, I shall destroy their city and everyone in it.'

Well, Jonah didn't want to go and warn them. He secretly wanted God to destroy them. And he knew that if they were sorry and changed their ways, then God wouldn't destroy them. And they deserved to be destroyed! They were real bullies! It would serve them right!

Hands up if you can sympathise with how Jonah was feeling – if you understand how he felt. I can understand how he felt. But imagine for a moment how *you'd* feel if you knew someone really hated you, for whatever reason. That would be awful. We want people to like us, don't we? Not hate us.

Well, Jonah went off to the harbour like God told him to. But he kept thinking, '*Shan't* go to Nineveh! *Shan't* go!' So he got on board a ship that was going in the opposite direction!

Draw Jonah sleeping.

He crept down below deck and fell fast asleep.

Draw clouds.

Pretty soon the sky got dark and there was a storm. The wind was really fierce. . .

Draw waves.

. . .and the waves were enormous.

The ship was thrown all over the place, and it began to fill up with water. The sailors were scared.

The captain woke Jonah up and said, 'God must be very angry with someone on this ship, because he's about to make it sink!' Jonah said, 'Oh no! It's me he's angry with. He told me to go to Nineveh, but I'm running away. There's only one thing you can do to save your ship, and that is to throw me overboard!'

Draw legs.

So the sailors threw Jonah into the deep, deep sea, and he was sure he was going to drown.

Draw face on fish and bubbles.

And that's when the great big fish came along and swallowed up Jonah.

Draw Jonah sitting inside fish.

It was dark and revolting inside the fish, but at least Jonah was still alive. So he thanked God for saving his life, and he said, 'Oh, all right then, I *will* go to Nineveh, if I must!'

After three days, God made the fish sick Jonah up onto the beach. Not a pretty sight! And off he went to Nineveh.

Draw crowd's heads and Jonah preaching.

He gathered all the Assyrians together and gave them the message from God. He said, 'You'd better watch out because, 40 days from now, Nineveh's going to be destroyed because of all the dreadful things you're doing.'

And guess what! The people stopped being violent and horrible, and they said 'sorry' to God. And sure enough, God forgave them, and didn't destroy them after all. By sending Jonah, he had given them a second chance.

The Bible teaches that by sending Jesus to this earth 2,000 years ago. . .

Draw cross.

. . .to die on a cross, God has given everyone a second chance – because

Jesus suffered in our place for the wrong things we've done, which the Bible calls SIN. Christians believe that if we say 'sorry' to God and decide to change our ways, like the people of Nineveh did, then God will forgive us too, and we'll be able to live with him for ever in heaven.

But Jonah was furious with God. He said, 'I *knew* you'd do this! I *knew* you'd be kind! I just knew it! It's not fair!' And he went into a sulk.

But God said to Jonah, 'Hey, wait a minute – I rescued *you* the other day, remember? I gave *you* a second chance when you disobeyed me. So why shouldn't I rescue the Assyrians too?' Jonah didn't have an answer to that one.

I just want to leave you with this thought. The Bible tells us that God hates (*add 's' to hate*) SIN – not just some sin, but all sin – and God loves (*add 's' to love*) PEOPLE – not just some people, but all people. And, although it's difficult sometimes, he wants us to do the same.

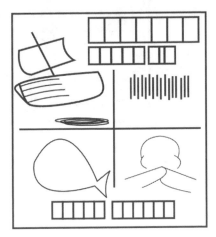

SUGGESTED SONGS:
I am listening to God (94)
We must be strong (226)
What a whale of a tale (229)

SUGGESTED PRAYER:
Thank you, Father, that you care not only for me, but also for this world. Help me to know when you are speaking to me, and give me the strength and courage not to run away from you, but to follow your instructions. Amen.

RUNNING WILD

VALUES: Courage; Hope

BIBLE REFERENCE: John 8:34–36

TEACHING POINT: True freedom comes from God.

NOTES: This talk is more suitable for older juniors. Instructions are provided for the use of a sketch-board – the ladder letter words are underlined.

YOU WILL NEED: Prepared sketch-board and paints, PowerPoint or OHP acetate and pens (see introductory section on ladder lettering or visit **www.canicholls.com** and **www.childrensministry.co.uk** for information on how to purchase downloads).

Draw in the word <u>WILD</u>.

Can anyone tell me what the word 'wild' means?

Let one or two children give you an answer.

Wild is when things are out of control. When there are storms and gales and torrential rain, we say the weather is wild. Wild is the opposite of tame. If you've got pet cats or dogs at home, they are tame – but tigers in the jungle are wild. Even if they're in a zoo, they are still wild animals.

Do you know what the fastest animal on earth is? It's the cheetah.

Draw in the word <u>RUNNING</u> in front of WILD.

The cheetah loves to run. But when it's locked up in a zoo, it can only run round and round in circles, going nowhere.

Today I want to tell you the true story of a young man who was out of control and running wild, but who was also running round and round in circles, going nowhere. His name is Nicky Cruz. He was brought up in the West Indies in the 1950s, in a family of 17. His parents didn't show him any love or respect. Most of the time, they just ignored him. His most vivid childhood memory was when someone caught him stealing at the age of five, and his dad locked him up in a dark place. Nicky started to feel <u>ANGER</u>.

By the time Nicky was 15 he had become uncontrollable, and so his parents sent him to America to live with one of his older brothers in New York. But Nicky didn't stay with his brother for long. He got excluded from school for fighting, and joined one of the many teenage gangs in New York. He lived a life of violence and crime. The gangs got money by stealing and mugging people. They had lots of fights with other gangs, and they were always running away from the police. Nicky didn't care about anything or anyone. People were frightened of him, and he soon became the leader of his gang of over 200 teenagers.

Nicky became close friends with another boy in the gang, and this was the first real friend he'd ever had in his whole life. Then, one day, his friend was killed by a rival gang. Nicky was terribly upset. And he also realised that *he* could easily end up the same way. First he began to feel <u>LONELY</u>, because all he had in his life was his anger and his hate. And then, when he woke up in the middle of the night, he began to feel <u>FEAR</u>. He knew he was always running but going nowhere.

After Nicky had been with his gang for three years, a Christian man called David came to New York to talk to the gangs about the love of God. David was physically small and weak. But he was extremely brave, because he was willing to take the risk of speaking to crowds of violent gang members on street corners when most people tried to avoid them!

One day David met Nicky, the terrifying gang leader. Which one do you think had the most power?

David had no power of his own, of course, but he knew he had <u>AUTHORITY</u> from God. God's power was inside him, and many young people actually left their gangs and gave their lives to Jesus. All Nicky did was get angry and threaten David, but David just responded to him with <u>LOVE</u>.

One night, David held a big meeting for thousands of gang members in a sports stadium. Nicky went along in order to make fun of him. But that night Nicky experienced something he'd not known before – the love of God – and suddenly he realised that Jesus had died so that all the dreadful things he'd done as a gang leader could be completely forgiven. He gave his life to Jesus that night, and became a Christian. At that moment he felt real joy for the first time, and a huge sense of <u>FREEDOM</u>.

After that, Nicky left his gang and went to a Christian college. He got married and had children. He returned to New York for a while to help gang members in trouble and drug addicts, and then he went to California to set up a project to help poor children.

Draw in the cross.

Through Nicky's work, lots of people's lives have been turned around dramatically – just like Nicky's own life had been turned around – from ANGER to AUTHORITY . . . from LONELINESS to LOVE . . . and from FEAR to FREEDOM.

Nicky's life has been far more exciting and worthwhile – and *enjoyable* – since he has been using God's authority rather than his own angry power which had only ever destroyed things.

All a cheetah in a zoo can do is run round and round in circles.

Paint in <u>FREE</u>.

But when it's set free into its proper environment – just watch it go!

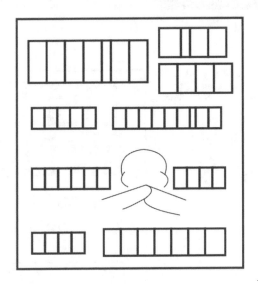

SUGGESTED SONGS:
Be bold, be strong (11)
I once was frightened of spiders (100)
2,000 years on (217)

SUGGESTED PRAYER:
Dear heavenly Father, help me through times of anger, loneliness and fear. Help me to put my trust in your authority and to know the true freedom that comes only from you. Amen.

SAMANTHA: A FRIEND OF JESUS

Lies   Steal
Cheat   Fight

VALUES: Forgiveness; Friendship

BIBLE REFERENCES: John 4:1–29; Psalm 139

TEACHING POINT: God knows all about us.

NOTES: Instructions are provided for the use of a sketch-board – the ladder letter words are underlined.

YOU WILL NEED: Prepared sketch-board and paints, PowerPoint or OHP acetate and pens (see introductory section on ladder lettering or visit **www.canicholls.com** and **www.childrensministry.co.uk** for information on how to purchase downloads).

I want to tell you the story of a girl named Samantha. Now, don't look round because it isn't anyone here!

What Samantha wanted more than anything else in the world was a friend. She was only five years old and really quite shy. When she started school she found it difficult to speak to the other boys and girls, and hardly anyone ever spoke to her because they thought, 'Well, if she isn't going to speak to me then I'm not going to speak to her!' And so it went on.

Sometimes, boys and girls, when we want something so badly, we can go about trying to get it in the wrong way. And eventually Samantha was so desperate to make some friends that she started to tell *(underline the word 'lies')* lies.

She stood up in class one day and told everyone about a new swimming pool that was being built in her back garden! Well, of course everybody wanted to know her now. One day during the summer when it was very hot, some children from her class came up to her and said, 'Sam, as it's so hot today, could we come over to your house this evening and play in your swimming pool?' Samantha had to think very quickly and she said, 'Oh, you can't this evening because Mum and Dad are having friends round.' This went on for some time until a group of children from her class grew suspicious. They followed her home without her knowing, and when they looked over her garden wall they could see – just as they had guessed – that Samantha had been telling lies.

Well, Sam was back to square one with no friends, because no one wants to be friends with a person who is always telling lies. 'What can I do now?' thought Sam. 'I know, I'll take a whole load of sweets to school and then people will like me.' In the playground it was great. Everybody gathered round, and Sam felt really special. 'Can I have one of your sweets, Sam? I'll be your friend!' There were so many people that it wasn't long before all Sam's sweets had gone. Sam didn't get much pocket money. What could she do now to get more sweets? That's when she started to *(underline the word 'steal')* steal.

When the coast was clear she looked inside her mum's purse and, without her mum knowing, she took some money and bought more sweets. Then, the next day, she went into the sweet shop and, when the shopkeeper wasn't looking, she stuffed her pockets with as many sweets as she could.

Do you know, boys and girls, the Bible teaches this: 'Be sure your sin will find you out.' In other words, if you are doing something you know you shouldn't be doing and you don't stop, there will come a time when you will get found out.

One day Sam did get caught and, boy, did she get into trouble big time! Her mum stopped all her pocket money for a very long time and she was grounded.

As you can guess, Sam was back to square one again with no friends.

'What can I do now to get some friends?' she thought. 'I know what! I'll be the cleverest person in the class!' And she started to *(underline the word 'cheat')* cheat.

She sat next to someone in class who was very clever, and she looked over their shoulder and she started to copy their work. It wasn't long before Sam was getting 9/10 and 10/10 for her sums and spelling. 'Oh you're so clever!' people would say to Sam. 'Would you help me with my homework?' But Sam wasn't very good with homework, and it wasn't long before all the girls and boys were getting things wrong and the teacher did some investigation and Sam was found out. She was told off and made to sit all on her own.

You don't like people copying your work do you? No. So do you think she had many friends now? *Wait for children to respond.*

As Samantha got a bit older she thought, 'I know! If they won't be friends with me because they *want* to, then I'll *make* them be friends with me!' So off she went to the gym and started to build up her muscles until she was stronger than anyone else in her class. Then she went round to people in the school saying, 'If you won't be in my gang, I'll punch you on the nose!' Soon everybody was Sam's friend – not because they really liked her – deep down they all thought she was stupid and silly – but because they didn't want to get into a *(underline the word 'fight')* fight with her. Even the Year Six boys were afraid of her!

Sam spent most of her school life lying, stealing, cheating and fighting. When the time came for her to leave school, do you know what? She didn't have a true friend in the whole world. Even though she was now a grown-up woman living in a village, no one wanted to know her. Everyone kept well away. Nobody could see that, deep down inside, Sam was really just a very lonely person who wanted someone to love her as a true friend.

Now, I must admit that I have made up Samantha's name because the Bible doesn't tell us her real name. And I've made up the story so far, to bring it up to date for you. Because in the time that Samantha lived – 2,000 years ago – they didn't have things like swimming pools. In fact, if you wanted water, you had to walk some distance to a well. In the Bible story that I have taken this from, women would go to the well in the morning or in the evening. The middle of the day would just be too hot. But the other women in the village didn't want Samantha with them and so she had to go and get her water in the middle of the day when the sun was at its hottest.

One day Samantha was at the well getting some water when a man asked her for a drink. This was really strange because men would never go to the well to fetch water in the middle of the day – or at any other time. They were far too lazy to get involved with things like that! 'Could I have a drink please?' the man asked. Samantha couldn't make it out. No one ever wanted to speak to her! And to hide her embarrassment she started to make fun of the man. To her surprise, the man wasn't nasty back. He just carried on talking to her. As he went on talking, Samantha's face started to change. First of all it went like this. . .

Paint in a shocked face.

. . .shocked! You see, this man knew all about Samantha and everything she had ever done. He knew all about her lying, stealing, cheating and fighting. When she thought about this, her face changed again. It went like this. . .

Paint in a sad face.

She went from looking rather shocked to feeling very sad. 'If he knows about all the rotten things I've done, he'll hate me just like everyone else does. Also, if he knows everything about me, then God must know everything about me and he won't like me either.'

I wonder if anyone can tell me who Samantha was speaking to?

Allow some of the children to respond. There are usually one or two who guess correctly, but it doesn't matter if they don't.

Let's see if you are right. If you are, it should fit in here: <u>JESUS</u>.

Do you think Jesus went away? No, of course he didn't. He carried on talking to her and told her that if she wanted to, she could become <u>A FRIEND OF JESUS</u>.

Now, the Bible teaches that when we become friends with Jesus, we become friends with God. The Bible also teaches that although God doesn't love some of the things we do, he still loves us and wants to be friends.

Now, how could God be friends with someone like Samantha who had behaved so badly and done lots of naughty things? Well, that's where Jesus comes into the picture. The Bible teaches that God loves us all and doesn't want us to get into trouble. So he sent Jesus to die on a cross to take the punishment for us – so that people like Samantha, and people like you and me, can be friends with God and live with him for ever.

When Samantha realised that God really loved her and wanted to be her friend, then for the first time in her life she started to do this:

Paint in a happy face.

She started to smile!

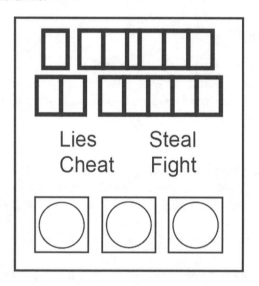

Lies   Steal
Cheat   Fight

SUGGESTED SONGS:
Father God, I wonder (43)
God is good (56)
There are hundreds of sparrows (206)

SUGGESTED PRAYER:
Dear Father, you know all about me and nothing is hidden from you. Help me to understand that with Jesus as my friend I do not have to pretend or try to impress anyone. Thank you that you are always willing to forgive me when I do bad things. Please show me where you want me to change for the better in order that I may do things that make you smile. Amen.

SIGNS OF THE TIMES

VALUE: Choosing right

BIBLE REFERENCE: Romans 8:1

TEACHING POINT: There is now no condemnation for those who are in Christ.

NOTES: This talk is geared towards older juniors. You will need to be sensitive when talking about death, as it is possible that some of the children may have suffered the loss of a close relative. Also, because the talk is quite directly evangelistic, always start with a sentence such as: 'I would like to talk to you about something that the Bible teaches and Christians believe.' In this way you will stay within the law, but at the same time allow the Holy Spirit to do what you cannot. Instructions are provided for the use of a sketch-board – the ladder letter words are underlined.

YOU WILL NEED: Prepared sketch-board and paints, PowerPoint or OHP acetate and pens (see introductory section on ladder lettering or visit **www.canicholls.com** and **www.childrensministry.co.uk** for information on how to purchase downloads).

How many of you come to school on a bicycle or ride your bike on the road?

Allow time for the children to respond.

Today we are going to find out how good we are with <u>SIGNS</u>. It's amazing how many people don't know their road signs. I will draw one here. See if you can guess what it is.

Draw in the 'roundabout' sign and allow the children to respond.

Yes, it's the sign for a roundabout. Now, the roundabout sign is interesting because it reminds me of <u>LIFE</u>. It reminds me of life because: we get up in the morning and we have a wash and we eat our breakfast. Then, after breakfast, we go to school and we work hard. And after school we go home and we have our tea and we go out to play and we go back indoors and we do our homework. Then after that we watch the telly or we play computer games and then we go to bed. Something like that, anyway. And do you know what? The next day we get up and do it all over again! For some people life can be like a roundabout – doing the same things day after day after day. At times we can feel that we are just going round and round in circles. Do you ever feel like that?
What about my next sign – who can tell me what this one is?

Draw in the 'dead end' sign and allow the children to respond.

Yes, it's the sign for a dead end. Have you ever had one of those days when everything seems to go wrong? Or maybe you have had a problem that you just couldn't solve. I have problems all the time and I have found that it's good if you've got lots of friends who can help you, especially when you feel you have come to a dead end in trying to sort something out.

Give a personal illustration if possible.

But if a 'roundabout' sign can remind us of life, what can a 'dead end' sign remind us of?

Allow the children to respond.

Yes, it can remind us of <u>DEATH</u>. Not a very happy subject to talk about, but it is a fact of life and something that happens to us all at some point. It can also be very sad for us when we lose someone close to us. But one thing I have learnt from Jesus through reading my Bible is that we never have to be afraid of death. I will show you why.

Who can tell me what this sign means?

Draw in the 'no entry' sign and allow the children to respond.

Yes, it's the sign for no entry. If I am driving my car and I see a road with a 'no entry' sign, it means I can't go into that road. The Bible teaches that we all have a problem, and because of this problem there is a 'no entry' sign to this place here.

Point to the place where you are going to put in the word 'heaven', but don't put it in just yet.

However, if we can remove the problem, then there is a completely different sign that is appropriate. Can anyone tell me what this sign is?

Draw in the national speed sign and allow the children to respond.

Yes, it's the national speed sign and it means that it is safe to travel at the fastest speed allowed. For example, if I am travelling along a motorway at 70 miles an hour, I may see a sign telling me that my lane is closed because of a hazard up ahead, and I have to move out of that lane and slow down. But once I get past the hazard, I will see this sign again and it means that I am free to go at the top speed again, with no restrictions.

Does anyone think they can guess what this word is going to be?

Allow two or three children to respond, and continue as appropriate.

See if you can guess as I put the letters in: <u>HEAVEN</u>. The Bible teaches that when I die I can go and live for ever with Jesus in heaven. But I have to get rid of the 'no entry' sign first in order that I am free to go in. How do I do that?

First we have got to understand what the problem is. The Bible tells us that the problem we all have is this:

Change the word 'SIGNS' into 'SINS' by obliterating the 'G'. Talk about sin, i.e. bad thoughts, words and deeds, etc.

Sin is like a hazard on the road that needs to be dealt with. If there is an accident involving lorries and cars, what people do we need to help sort out the mess?

Allow some of the children to respond.

Yes, we need the help of experts like the police, fire-fighters and paramedics who know what they are doing. Now, the problem of sin can make a big mess of our lives, and so we need an expert who can sort out all that mess.

The Bible teaches that 2,000 years ago Jesus came to this earth and showed us how we should live our lives, and he dealt with sin once and for all when he died on the cross. That's because when he suffered and died, he was taking the punishment that we deserve for all the bad things we do in our lives. So, whenever someone decides to follow Jesus and become his friend and put their trust in him, the 'no entry' sign is removed from heaven and that person is free to go in.

I have one more sign. Can anyone tell me what this sign is?

Draw in the 'crossroads' sign and let the children respond.

Yes, it's the sign for a crossroads. Can anyone tell me what you have to do when you see a crossroads sign?

Let the children respond.

One of the things you have to do at a crossroads is make a decision – which road are you going to take? And when people hear about Jesus and what Jesus has done for them, it is like coming to a crossroads in life and a decision has to be made about which way to go. That decision, of course, is yours.

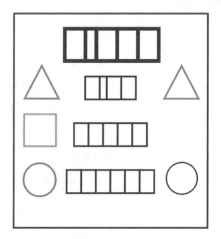

SUGGESTED SONGS:
Be still (13)
One in a million (168)

SUGGESTED PRAYER:
Dear Father, life can so often take us down different roads with twists and turns and hazards that can cause so many problems. Please surround me with good friends and, whenever I am faced with a difficult choice, help me always to make the right decision. Amen.

SINK OR SWIM?

VALUES: Humility; Trust

BIBLE REFERENCE: James 1:2–3

TEACHING POINT: Jesus will never let us down.

NOTES: Instructions are provided for the use of a sketch-board – the ladder letter words are underlined.

YOU WILL NEED: Prepared sketch-board and paints, PowerPoint or OHP acetate and pens (see introductory section on ladder lettering or visit **www.canicholls.com** and **www.childrensministry.co.uk** for information on how to purchase downloads).

I would like to ask you a question. Are you UNSINKABLE?

There are a lot of people in the world today who think they are unsinkable and unstoppable, and nothing or no one is going to get in their way. I am sure you are not like that, but there are some people who like to give that impression.

Do you like history lessons, girls and boys? Well, one of the great things about history is that you can learn an awful lot from other people's mistakes. For example, what about this one?

Draw in the rest of the ship.

Can anyone tell me what this is? This was a very famous ship that hit an iceberg in the year 1912 and sank. It had 2,224 passengers on board, of which 1,513 lost their lives. Only 711 people survived. Can anyone tell me the name of the ship?

To its passengers, the Titanic seemed very SAFE. People were told that it was unsinkable. It was solid. It was powerful. And it became familiar to the passengers. It was their comfortable home for the journey across the Atlantic – especially if you happened to be travelling first class!

Now, our lives can be like that. They seem so permanent, don't they? Our surroundings, like this school, are familiar to us. And we think we can rely on ourselves, even if we can't always rely on other people.

But think about this. Just how safe was the Titanic? As it set out across the Atlantic. . .

Draw iceberg.

. . .that famous iceberg was already on its journey from the frozen north. The course and speed of the ship, together with the weather conditions, meant that the ship and the iceberg were bound to collide at a particular time and place.

Draw in the rest of the sinking ship.

When that happened, the passengers couldn't believe that their solid surroundings were going to vanish beneath their feet within an hour or so. There was even a group of musicians on deck playing music, to try and create the illusion of normality!

Now I want you to think about your life, with all its routines. You get up, you come to school, you go home, you have your tea, you watch telly or play on the computer, and then you go to bed. The next day you do it all over again, and your life seems very secure.

The thing is, girls and boys, you never know when you are going to be hit by a big problem. But you can be <u>CERTAIN</u> that sooner or later it will happen. We are all hit by problems from time to time, some bigger than others. But when we are hit, do we sink or do we swim? Do we handle the problem, or do we give in?

For instance, there might come a time in your life when you are tempted to take drugs. If that happens, will you be able to say 'No' and swim away to safety? Or will you say 'Yes' and sink with the problem?

Very many people went down with the Titanic. Those who survived that disaster only survived because they had the help of a lifeboat. The trouble was, there were not enough lifeboats to go round. The designers of the Titanic had decided that having the right number of lifeboats on deck would look messy, and they wanted the ship to look cool.

There is a word on the board/screen that will cause us to sink every time we are hit by a problem. Can you see what it is? It's a bit like a word-search.

Wait a short while to see if anyone can answer, then circle the word 'SIN' in the middle of 'UNSINKABLE'. Define sin in a way that is relevant to children.

Sin is like a heavy weight that is padlocked to our legs, and it will always stop us from swimming in times of trouble. In order to undo a padlock, you need to have a key. The Bible teaches, and Christians believe, that there *is* a key. It might look like a strange key to you. . .

Draw the cross.

. . .but it's a key that I have found to work very well.

Here you can give a gospel message, and talk about Jesus being the key. Give a personal testimony if you wish, but always keep it relevant to the age of the children.

They thought it wasn't cool to have too many lifeboats on the Titanic because it didn't look good. Some people might not think it's cool to follow Jesus. But Jesus has never let me down. He helps me in every situation in life, and he is the coolest person to have around whenever I hit a problem. He is like a lifeboat, and he is my <u>SECURITY</u> in times of trouble.

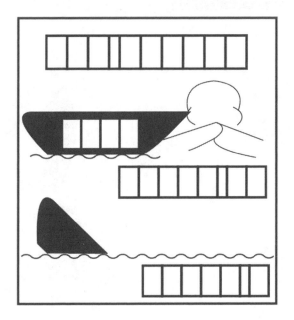

SUGGESTED SONGS:
Don't worry (37)
God knows the things we really need (59)

SUGGESTED PRAYER:
Dear Father in heaven, the Bible says it is not *if* we face trials or problems, but *when*. Help me through those times that seem impossible, and help me to remember that with you I can be unsinkable. Amen.

SKINNY DIPPING

VALUE: Obedience

BIBLE REFERENCES: 2 Kings 5:1–16; 2 Corinthians 5:17

TEACHING POINT: God has a plan for our lives.

YOU WILL NEED: Prepared illustrations on OHP acetates or PowerPoint (visit **www.canicholls.com** and **www.childrensministry.co.uk** for information on how to purchase downloads).

It all happened many years ago, long before Jesus was born.

Show picture of Izzy.

An army from Syria invaded Israel, and a little girl (who I've called Izzy), was taken from her home and made to work as a slave. She worked in the home of a very important soldier – he was the commander of the Syrian army – and his name was Naaman. The king of Syria liked Naaman because he was a brave and clever man and led the army to win many battles.

Show picture of Izzy and Mrs Naaman.

One day little Izzy saw that Mrs Naaman was looking sad and crying, and so she asked her why. 'It's my husband,' said Mrs Naaman. 'He got out of bed this morning and noticed that he had this awful skin disease called leprosy, and I'm afraid that he is going to die.'

Now, I used to have a really awful disease too. It wasn't leprosy, it was called 'I' disease. Do you know what 'I' disease is? I will tell you. It's '*I* want this, *I* want that, and *I* want it now!' More about that later.

Did you know, children, that people who have leprosy lose all the feeling in their skin and muscles, especially of their hands, feet and face, and this means that they can easily hurt themselves very badly indeed without realising it. Even today, if this disease is not dealt with in the early stages, it can be disastrous. People don't actually die from leprosy, but Mrs Naaman didn't know that, and she was beside herself with worry.

Show picture of Naaman.

Little Izzy said to Mrs Naaman, 'If only Commander Naaman would go and see this man I know in Israel. His name is Mr Elisha. He is a great man of God. He often helps people when they are sick. I am sure that if Commander Naaman were to go and see him, he would be able to help him.'

Show picture of Naaman and king.

When Naaman got to hear of this Mr Elisha, he went to the king and asked for permission to go to Israel to see him. Well, of course the king wanted Naaman to get better, so he gave his permission.

Show picture of sad Naaman.

Naaman set off to see Mr Elisha, but he made a few mistakes along the way.

The first thing he did wrong was to take money to pay for his healing. The Bible teaches that when God does anything for anyone, he does it because he loves them and not because he wants paying for it.

The next mistake that Naaman made was to go to the wrong person. He thought to himself, 'Surely if God is going to use anyone to help me, he is going to use someone really important, because I am such an important person. I know,' he thought, 'I will go and see the king of Israel!' So when he arrived in Israel, he went to where the king lived and he knocked at the door. 'I have come to see the king!' he said. When the king saw Naaman, he said, 'What can I do for you?' 'I've got leprosy,' said Naaman, 'and I want you to cure me and make me well!' The king went red with embarrassment, because Naaman was asking him to do something he knew he couldn't do. Then the king got angry and started jumping up and down and shouting at Naaman. He did all this to hide his embarrassment.

The Bible teaches that God doesn't just use the people we think are important. To God we are all as important as each other, and he likes to use ordinary people like you and me to help others.

In the end, Naaman thought he had better do what he had been advised to do in the first place, and go and see this Mr Elisha.

When Naaman eventually arrived at Mr Elisha's house, he knocked at the door.

Show picture of servant and Naaman.

After a while, Mr Elisha's servant opened the door. 'Yes, what can I do for you?' he said. 'I'm Commander Naaman, and I have come to see Mr Elisha to ask him to cure my leprosy.' 'Oh yes,' said the servant, 'Mr Elisha was told that you would be turning up, and he has told me to tell you to go and wash yourself in the river Jordan seven times!' And with that he shut the door!

Naaman was absolutely furious. 'I'm an important man! Surely Mr Elisha should have come to see me himself, and waved his hand over my leprosy and called on his God to cure me? Instead of that he sends out his little servant to tell me to go and wash in that dirty old river Jordan! There are rivers back home in Syria far better than the Jordan!'

Naaman really didn't like being told what to do. He wanted to do things his own way. Often we can make a mistake when we do things our way and not God's way. The Bible teaches, and Christians believe, that God's plan for us is to follow Jesus – but many people don't like that idea.

Well, Naaman jumped back into his chariot, his face looking like a big red tomato! He was so angry!

But as he was driving off along the dusty road, he began to calm down and he thought, 'I suppose I might as well give it a try – just in case it works. You never know!'

Show picture of Naaman in river.

And so he waded out into the river Jordan, up to his middle, and started to dip himself under the water – one, two, three, four, five, six times. 'Oh, this is stupid!' he thought. 'Nothing's happening.' He was about to climb out of the river, but then he thought, 'Perhaps I should do *exactly* as I was told.'

Show picture of Naaman happy.

So he went under the water for the seventh time and this time, when he came up, he couldn't believe his eyes! All his leprosy had vanished and his skin looked and felt perfect and like new again!

Show picture of Naaman and Elisha.

Naaman was so excited. He went back as fast as he could to Mr Elisha's house and knocked on the door. This time Mr Elisha himself opened the door. 'Thank you so much, Mr Elisha! I'm so pleased I did what I was told to do. Now I know there is no God in all the land like the God you serve here in Israel.' Naaman went away a very happy man.

Show picture of cross.

The Bible teaches that God has a plan for all of us. He wants to cure us of our 'I' disease. *(Elaborate if you wish.)* And he wants us to ask Jesus to be our friend so that we can live with him for ever in heaven. I wonder what you will do?

SUGGESTED SONGS:
God is good (56)
He's got the whole wide world (86)
I can't stop (98)

SUGGESTED PRAYER:
Forgive me, Father, when I don't always do things your way. Thank you for having a plan for my life. Help me to understand that your way is best. Amen.

SMALL MAN, BIG CHANGE...

VALUES: Saying sorry; Sharing

BIBLE REFERENCE: Luke 19:1–10

TEACHING POINT: Jesus came to seek and save the lost.

YOU WILL NEED: Prepared illustrations on OHP acetates or PowerPoint (visit **www.canicholls.com** and **www.childrensministry.co.uk** for information on how to purchase downloads).

I would like to tell you today about a man from the Bible whose life was turned completely upside down when he met Jesus.

Greedy! He was very greedy and he didn't like to share! In fact he was so greedy, if he'd had a bag of toffees when he was at school, he would have been able to unwrap a toffee in his pocket with one hand and put it in his mouth with no one seeing. And do you know what he loved more than anything else in the world? *Money!* He was very selfish. He didn't like to give anything to anyone, he only liked to take, take, take.

His name was Zacchaeus, and he was a chief tax collector. *(Explain what this means.)* And he was ever so rich. *(Explain why, e.g. because he cheated people, etc.)*

The Bible teaches that when we do wrong things like steal and cheat, not only do we hurt others but we also hurt God.

Lonely! Put your hands up, boys and girls, if you have ever felt sad and lonely.

Zacchaeus certainly knew what it was like to be sad and lonely. No one wanted to be his friend. He would stand on the street and wave to people, but no one would bother to wave back. Nobody liked Zacchaeus. But God loved Zacchaeus. He didn't like what Zacchaeus did, but he did love him and wanted to be his friend. God doesn't like it when we steal and cheat, but he does love us. And just like he wanted to be Zacchaeus's friend, the Bible tells us that he wants to be our friend too.

Show picture of Jesus addressing crowd.

One day, Jesus was visiting Jericho, the town where Zacchaeus lived. People gathered round to hear what Jesus had to say. Zacchaeus tried to get a look at Jesus, but he was just too small, and people kept pushing him to the back of the crowd. 'Go away, Zacchaeus!' they would say. 'We don't like you. And what's more, Jesus wouldn't like you either. So go away!'

Then Zacchaeus had an idea.

Show picture of Zacchaeus beginning to climb tree.

Zacchaeus thought to himself, 'If I can climb this tree, I will be higher than anyone else and I'll be able to see Jesus!' And so that's what Zacchaeus did.

Show picture of Zacchaeus sitting in the tree.

Today, if people want to get to know Jesus, they don't have to climb trees. What the Bible teaches, and what Christians believe, is that all we need to do is say 'sorry' to God and ask Jesus to be our friend – and he will.

I don't suppose it was easy for Zacchaeus to climb that tree – he only had short arms and legs – but eventually he made it. Now he could see Jesus, but. . .

Show picture of Zacchaeus from Jesus' point of view.

. . .Jesus could also see Zacchaeus.

Jesus said to the crowd, 'Who's the little man up that tree?' 'Oh, that's Zacchaeus,' somebody said. 'He's the local tax collector. You wouldn't want to know him.' Jesus said, 'But I *do* want to know him!' Jesus made his way through the crowd to the tree Zacchaeus had climbed.

Show picture of Jesus looking up at Zacchaeus.

Looking up, he said, 'Zacchaeus, I would like to come to your house for tea!' Well, that made Zacchaeus feel really special. In fact, Zacchaeus was so surprised that Jesus wanted to come to his house. . .

Show picture of Zacchaeus hanging upside-down from branch.

. . .that he nearly fell out of the tree!

Show picture of Jesus and Zacchaeus going into his house.

When the people of the town saw Jesus going home with Zacchaeus, they didn't like it one bit. 'Look at that!' they said. 'He's going to the house of a sinner, that horrible little man Zacchaeus!'

But the Bible teaches, boys and girls, that Jesus came into this world to help people like Zacchaeus – people who have lost their way. The Bible teaches that Jesus came to seek and to save the lost.

Show picture of Jesus embracing Zacchaeus.

When Jesus was inside Zacchaeus's home, Zacchaeus said something that made Jesus really happy. He said, 'Jesus, I will give half my money to the poor.

And where I have taken £5 from anyone that I shouldn't have done, I will give them £20 back.'

Zacchaeus had decided to give up his love of money, because he realised he loved Jesus and he loved God far more than money. He had become a completely changed man, and his life had been turned upside-down. Or, rather, it had at long last been turned *the right way up!*

SUGGESTED SONG:
Blessed be the name of the Lord (19)
Zacchaeus (161)

SUGGESTED PRAYER:
Dear Father, I am sorry if I have done anything that offends you and hurts others. Teach me your ways and give me the courage to put things right where I can. Amen.

THE CIRCLE OF LIFE

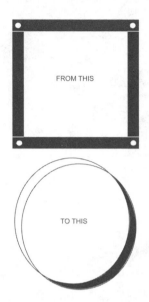

FROM THIS

TO THIS

VALUES: Choosing right; Obedience

BIBLE REFERENCES: Deuteronomy 4:29; Matthew 7:7; John 11:25

TEACHING POINT: God's way is perfect and leads to eternal life.

NOTES: This talk is aimed at older children in Key Stage 2, and would be especially appropriate at the end of the school year. If your timing is right at the end of the talk, this object lesson will be visually very effective.

YOU WILL NEED: One Squircle. To make the 'Squircle' you will need four strips of strong card approximately 30 cm × 3 cm. Colour one green, one red, one blue and one gold or yellow. Punch a hole in both ends of each piece of card so that when they are held together by paper fasteners they will form a perfect square. This can also be done using four painted hacksaw blades riveted together. You will find that by holding two opposite sides and twisting them, the square will instantly turn into a circle.

Start by holding up the square with the green colour at the top.

Good morning, girls and boys. Today I would like to show you something with this circle.

The children will start to call out and tell you that it's a square.

Well the circle is hidden and you can't see it, but I promise you it's there. You only need to know the secret and keep looking. It reminds me that you can't see God, but the Bible teaches that he is there and that one day you will be able to see him – just like you will be able to see the circle if you keep looking. The Bible also teaches that if you seek God with all your heart, you will find him.

Anyway, back to my talk that I have entitled 'The Circle of Life'. The green reminds me of the fact that we start life at a very young age! And that we need to grow. That's why I have used the colour green because it reminds me of things that grow. It also reminds me that when you are young you have a lot to learn. However, when you are in Year Six you know a lot more than you did when you were in your first year at school. And so life goes on. We never really stop learning. Eventually/soon you will leave this school and you will go up a year and into another phase of life.

Turn the square so that the red colour is at the top.

Then you enter your teenage years. I have coloured this red because, although you are still learning, these can also be the rebellious years. Red reminds me of anger and danger. You can find yourself wanting to kick against the system and change things that you don't like. You are older, more confident and feeling that you have a voice that should be heard. That can be a good thing – but it can also be a bad thing.

Being rebellious, or rebelling against something, is when you deliberately want to go the opposite way to the way that is being suggested. For example, this school has rules, and if you purposely break those rules you are being rebellious in a bad way. However, it is also possible for you to be rebellious in a good way. How do you think that might be?

Allow two or three to answer, acknowledging and thanking them for their participation.

If you were with a group of people who wanted to do something that you knew was wrong – like taking drugs or bullying someone – but you didn't want to go along with it, you would be rebelling in a good way. Rebelling in a good way can take a lot of courage.

When we rebel against God by going our own way and not following his rules, the Bible calls it sin and says that it prevents us from having a relationship with God.

Turn the square so that the blue colour is at the top.

Eventually you will leave school, college or university and move into adult life. Many of you will get married and have children of your own, with all the responsibilities that go with family life. Many of you will have responsible jobs where you have to make tough decisions. Some of you may become teachers with the responsibility of helping others learn life's skills. One thing I have learnt, girls and boys, as I've got older, is that you can't lead or teach others unless you know what you are doing.

The Bible teaches that this is one of the reasons why God sent Jesus. Because, when it comes to the things of God, no one can teach them like Jesus can. But not only did Jesus come to teach us about God, he also came to pay the price for all our sin by dying on a cross. The Bible teaches that if we put our trust in Jesus, we can become friends with God. God will then forgive us for the rebellious things we have done that have separated us from him – which brings me to the last part of our journey round the circle of life.

Turn the square so that the gold or yellow colour is at the top.

Imagine that you have done all your growing, studying, working, leading and teaching others, and raising a family. You may have achieved your ambitions and have had all sorts of adventures and experiences, and faced all kinds of challenges along the way. And now you are old and are entering into what I call the golden years. I call them the golden years because, just as gold has to be refined – or purified – by fire, when we are old we have – hopefully – been refined by life and all the problems and troubles it has thrown at us. You might well think, 'What is the point of it all? What is the point of life? I have to go through all that hassle, and then I die!'

Many people do think that, but Christians think something else – because the Bible teaches, and Christians believe, that life doesn't end here. If we have put our trust in Jesus, then when we die. . .

Twist the sides of the square so that it is instantly transformed into a circle.

. . .we instantly change and enter into eternal life – a life, like this circle, that is never-ending.

SUGGESTED SONGS:
He's got the whole wide world (86)
Seek ye first (182)

SUGGESTED PRAYER:
Heavenly Father, help me as I grow to have the desire to work hard and to learn. Help me also to be rebellious in a good way, a way that helps not only me, but others too. Help me to understand and to remember that your way is perfect and leads to life eternal. Amen.

THE EASY WAY OUT

VALUES: Forgiveness; Honesty

BIBLE REFERENCES: Matthew 26:33–75; John 21:1–17

TEACHING POINT: Having the courage to be honest.

NOTE: Instructions are provided for the use of a sketch-board – the ladder letter words are underlined.

YOU WILL NEED: Prepared sketch-board and paints, PowerPoint or OHP acetate and pens (see introductory section on ladder lettering or visit **www.canicholls.com** and **www.childrensministry.co.uk** for information on how to purchase downloads).

Just supposing you got into trouble – would you look for this? The <u>EASY WAY OUT</u>. Did you know that what looks like the easy way out at the time, can be the most difficult way out in the end?

This is a story from the Bible about a man called Simon Peter, who tried to take the easy way out.

One evening, Jesus was having his very last meal with his twelve disciples. He said to them, 'Tonight, one of you is going to betray me and turn me in to the authorities, and I am going to be executed.'

Now, Simon Peter was one of Jesus' disciples.

Draw confident pin-man.

He said, 'Jesus, I'll never let you down! I'll lay down my life for you!' He was being <u>RASH</u>. That doesn't mean he had the measles and he'd come out in a rash! 'Rash' means saying something or doing something without thinking about it first. Simon Peter was like that.

Are you like that? Have you ever made a rash promise? For instance, put your hand up if you have ever made a New Year's resolution which you couldn't keep up after the 3rd of January.

Jesus knew what Simon Peter was like, and he said, 'Simon, let me tell you something. Before tomorrow morning when the cock crows, you're going to tell three people that you don't even know me!' Do you think Simon Peter believed that? I doubt it.

That night, the disciple called Judas *did* betray Jesus, and Jesus *was* arrested and taken to the high priest's house for his trial. Simon Peter followed at a distance and merged in with the crowds in the courtyard.

Draw despondent pin-man.

He was keeping his head down now. All his courage had gone. He was frightened of being arrested too. He was hoping no one would recognise him as being one of Jesus' friends. Then a servant stared at him and said in a loud voice so everyone could hear, 'He was with Jesus!' Simon Peter said, 'No I wasn't! I don't even know the man!'

Then someone else said, 'You're one of Jesus' friends!' Simon Peter said, 'No I'm not!' He was getting really panicky now. The night wore on, and then someone else said, 'I know you're one of Jesus' friends!' And Simon Peter said, '*No I'm not!* I don't know what you're talking about!'

Just then, the cock crowed, and Simon Peter remembered what Jesus had said. He left that courtyard crying bitterly. He felt <u>WRETCHED</u>. Today we might say he was 'gutted'. He had let his friend Jesus down, and he had let himself down too.

The next day. . .

Draw the cross.

. . .Jesus was crucified, even though he hadn't done anything wrong. The Bible tells us that when Jesus was crucified, he took the punishment for all the things we've ever done wrong, so that God can forgive us if we ask him to.

Just imagine how awful Simon Peter must have felt all this time. He didn't think he'd ever see Jesus again. Probably he couldn't eat or sleep for worrying about the lies he'd told. He had no peace. Anything would have been better than that.

The Bible tells us that three days later Jesus rose from the dead and that he is alive today.

Several days later, the disciples were in their boat fishing. They hadn't caught a single fish all night. At dawn, they saw a man on the beach. He shouted, 'Throw your net over the right-hand side of the boat!' So they did, and they caught so many fish that they couldn't pull the net in. They knew straight away that it was Jesus.

Simon Peter immediately jumped overboard – splash! – with all his clothes on, and swam as fast as he could to get to Jesus. Why do you think he was in such a hurry to get to Jesus? To make sure they were still friends.

Draw fire.

Jesus was very relaxed, and he cooked breakfast for the disciples.

Afterwards, he took Simon Peter on one side and said, 'Simon, do you love me more than you love anyone else?' Simon Peter said, 'Yes, you know I'm your friend.' So Jesus said something very strange, 'Then feed my sheep!' He didn't mean real sheep of course. Who do you think he meant by 'sheep'? He meant people. Take care of my people. So even though Simon Peter had let Jesus down, Jesus was giving him an important job to do.

Then Jesus said, 'Simon do you really love me?' Simon Peter said, 'Yes, you know I'm your friend.' So Jesus said, 'Then take care of my sheep!' Then a third time Jesus said, 'Simon, are you *really* my friend?' And Simon Peter said, 'You know my heart, Jesus, you know I am!' So Jesus said, 'Then feed my sheep!'

Draw elated pin-man.

Simon Peter must have been over the moon!

Why do you think Jesus asked Simon Peter the same question three times? It wiped out the three times Simon Peter had lied. Jesus was showing him that he was completely forgiven. Simon Peter had been <u>RESTORED</u>. 'Restored' means made like new again.

God knows that *we* will sometimes make mistakes. But the Bible says that when God sees that we're really sorry, then we only have to ask him and he will *always* forgive us and make **us** like new again, because he loves us, and because Jesus died in our place on the cross.

But Simon Peter had gone through a terrible time, all because he'd lied. So if you get into trouble, think about Simon Peter. And remember that the true easy way out, even if it doesn't seem like it at the time, is always this: <u>HONESTY</u>.

SUGGESTED SONGS:
For I'm building a people of power (48)
We must be strong (226)

SUGGESTED PRAYER:
Dear heavenly Father, please forgive me when I have lied in order to take the easy way out. Give me the courage to always be honest, no matter how difficult that might be. Amen.

THE GOSPEL IN A NUTSHELL

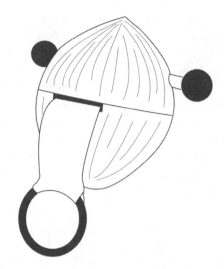

VALUES: Choosing right; Forgiveness

BIBLE REFERENCES: Genesis 1 – 3; 1 Peter 1:17–19

TEACHING POINT: The gospel message.

NOTES: The idea of using a nutshell with a multi-coloured ribbon for this talk has been around for years. There are many children's evangelists who will know of it. However, whenever I use my 'talking coconut' I am surprised how many people have never seen it. I have seen the prop for sale but, if you are unable to purchase one, they are quite simple to make. Take the time to make this prop, and you will have a visual aid that will last you a lifetime.

YOU WILL NEED: One prepared coconut with coloured ribbon in this order, starting with the first colour seen by the onlookers: yellow / black / red / white / green / yellow (see instructions at the end of this assembly or visit **www.canicholls.com**).

Start by asking the children if they have ever seen a talking coconut. Hold up your bag, saying that inside the bag you have a talking coconut! I have found this a great way to get the children's attention. Slowly take the coconut out of the bag.

You may never have seen a talking coconut before, but this is mine. It's got a message inside it, and it's all done with colours. If you listen really carefully, you may just hear it speaking to you! Can anybody guess the first colour?

Hold the coconut so that you are pulling the ribbon through your fingers. Always keep the next colour hidden until you are ready for it. I have found that asking the children to guess the colours before I show them, keeps the anticipation and involvement alive.

Pull out the yellow ribbon, stopping just before the black.

If you said 'yellow', then you were right. This is a bright colour and it reminds me of the beginning of the Bible where it talks about God creating the world and people. Everything was perfect. Can anyone tell me how many days the Bible says it took for God to make the world? *(Allow someone to answer.)*
Yes, it was six. And on the seventh day we are told that God rested.
And can anyone tell me the name of the first person who the Bible tells us God created? *(Allow someone to answer.)*
Yes, it was Adam. Now, Adam had a wife named Eve, and they seemed to be getting along really well. There was no lying, no stealing, no cheating, no bad words and no fighting. And the most important thing of all – they had a great relationship with God. That was until one day when Adam did something God had told him not to do. Now, be honest, have you ever done anything you know you shouldn't have done, and been punished for it? Well, both Adam and his wife, Eve, got punished.
Can anyone guess the next colour?

Pull out the black ribbon, stopping just before the red.

If you said 'black', then you were right. The Bible teaches that this was the first time anyone had disobeyed God, and sin entered the world. Sin is a terrible thing caused by our own selfish behaviour. 'Sin' is a small word, but it has big consequences – the worst being that it separates us from God. God loves us, but he will never have anything to do with sin. We are all very precious to God and he wants us to be perfect. It makes him so sad to see us ruining our lives by all our acts of selfish behaviour.

Let me give you an illustration. I wonder if anyone here collects coins? Now, serious coin collectors will only handle their coins if they have special gloves on. This is because the perfect mint condition of a coin can be spoilt once it comes into contact with even the tiniest amount of sweat or grease on our skin. Sin has the same effect on our lives. The Bible talks about it being like an indelible mark on us that we can never wash away – a mark that is not on the outside, but on the inside. It sounds almost hopeless, doesn't it? But with God there is always a way round – or should I say through – a problem. If you were to go to a printing factory or a garage, you would see the people who work there using special cleansing agents to remove the ink, oil or grease that had got right down into their skin. And the Bible teaches that we need a special cleansing agent to remove the stain that sin makes in our hearts.

Can anyone guess the next colour? Did I hear someone say 'red'?

Pull out the red ribbon, stopping just before the white.

If you said 'red', then you were right. The red ribbon reminds me of the special cleansing agent we need. The Bible talks about God sending Jesus to die on a cross so that my sin can be forgiven. It says that the blood of Jesus can make me right with God – because when Jesus died on the cross, he was taking the punishment for all my sin, past, present and future.

What it is also saying is that if I pray and ask Jesus to live in my heart, not only will he help me get rid of all my selfishness and do the things that make God happy, but that God will forgive me for all the naughty things I have done in the past. Then God no longer sees my sin, and he even chooses not to remember it anymore.

So can anyone tell me what the next colour is? Who said 'white'?

Pull out the white ribbon, stopping just before the green.

If you said 'white', you were right. Christians believe this is how God sees us if we ask his forgiveness and ask Jesus to live in our hearts. Jesus removes the horrible stain of sin. It is as though we had never sinned, and our friendship with God is made perfect again. He helps us not to tell lies, or steal, or cheat, or do all the naughty things we can do when we want to get our own way. And I have found that living God's way does make for a happier life.

So can anyone tell me what the next colour is? Who said 'green'?

Pull out the green ribbon, stopping just before the yellow.

If you said 'green', you were right. What does green make you think of, or remind you of? *(Allow some of the children to give you an answer.)*

The colour green makes me think of things that grow. And the Bible teaches that that is something I need to do as a Christian – to grow. Now, how do you think I can do that? *(Let some of the children answer if they wish.)*

In order for me to grow, I have to spend time getting to know God. I need to get to know the sort of things that God likes me to do, as well as the things he doesn't. I can do that by reading my Bible. I also go to church and meet up with other Christians who help me and encourage me. It's a little bit like going to school for an hour or so, but on a Sunday – not to learn how to do sums or spellings, but to learn about the things of God. I also pray to God. That just means talking to God, like you would to a close friend. In order to get to know someone really well, you have to spend time with that person. I have found that the more I do these things, the more I get to know God. And the more I get to know God, the more I grow as a Christian.

Can anyone tell me what the last colour is going to be?

Pull out the yellow ribbon.

How many of you said 'yellow'? If you said 'yellow', then you were right. This takes us right back to the beginning when everything was perfect before sin entered the world. The Bible teaches that when a Christian dies, he or she goes to live with God in heaven where everything is perfect. We are told there is no pain or suffering in heaven, and there are no tears. There is certainly no lying, stealing or cheating there, and everyone is surrounded by God's love. I don't know about you, but that sounds a pretty good place to me, and a place where I would want to live for ever. It's *good news*. In the Bible, the word for the good news about Jesus is 'gospel'.

And that, boys and girls, is what is known as 'the gospel in a nutshell'!

SUGGESTED SONGS:
Bind us together, Lord (18)
Lord, I lift your name on high (143)
Who's the king of the jungle? (239)

SUGGESTED PRAYER:
Dear Father in heaven, forgive me when I turn my back on you and go my own way. Help me to change and do the things that make you happy, not the things that make you sad. Amen.

Instructions for making the talking coconut

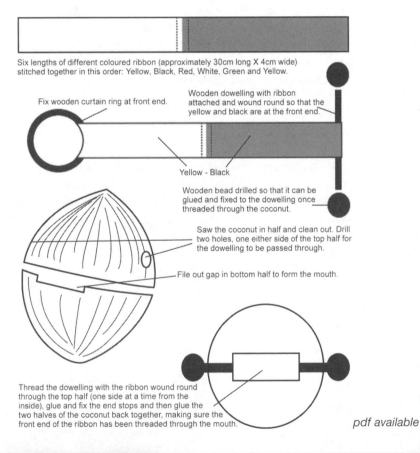

Six lengths of different coloured ribbon (approximately 30cm long X 4cm wide) stitched together in this order: Yellow, Black, Red, White, Green and Yellow.

Fix wooden curtain ring at front end.

Wooden dowelling with ribbon attached and wound round so that the yellow and black are at the front end.

Yellow - Black

Wooden bead drilled so that it can be glued and fixed to the dowelling once threaded through the coconut.

Saw the coconut in half and clean out. Drill two holes, one either side of the top half for the dowelling to be passed through.

File out gap in bottom half to form the mouth.

Thread the dowelling with the ribbon wound round through the top half (one side at a time from the inside), glue and fix the end stops and then glue the two halves of the coconut back together, making sure the front end of the ribbon has been threaded through the mouth.

pdf available

THE PUZZLE OF LIFE

VALUE: Responsibility

BIBLE REFERENCES: Luke 10:27; Matthew 7:25; Luke 6:42

TEACHING POINT: Look at the way you live – is it the best it could be?

NOTE: Instructions are provided for the use of a sketch-board – the ladder letter words are underlined.

YOU WILL NEED: Prepared sketch-board and paints, PowerPoint or OHP acetate and pens (see introductory section on ladder lettering or visit **www.canicholls.com** and **www.childrensministry.co.uk** for information on how to purchase downloads).

Do you like jigsaw puzzles, girls and boys? I do! I love trying to sort out all the bits and pieces. And eventually I manage to make some sense of what started out as a real mess.

Life is often a bit like a puzzle. Let's look at the word 'life'. There are different ways of looking at it. For example, some people look at life like this:

LIFE

They will take the letter 'i' in 'life' and make it the most important. They see themselves as a self-made trinity – me, myself and I. They don't care about anyone else. Tell me, girls and boys, do you think that is how God would want us to live? Of course not. Jesus was often telling people about how much they should care for others. Jesus would say that it is important to love God with all your heart, but it is also important to love the people around you as much as you love yourself. Sometimes that can be very difficult, especially if someone has done something to hurt you or upset you.

Let's look at another way that some people look at life. They look at it like this:

LIFE

These are the people who are always blaming others. They will never take responsibility for their own actions. They will always point the finger and say, 'If only he hadn't done that!' 'If only she hadn't said that!' 'It's their fault!' 'It's not my fault!' These people are always pointing the finger at other people and judging them.

Let's try a little experiment. I would like you all to point your finger at me, like this.

Point your finger at the children, and get them to do the same.

Now, with your finger pointed, I want you slowly to turn your hand over. How many fingers do you see pointing back at you? Yes, three. Often the problem is not with other people, but with ourselves. Jesus had something to say about this too. He said something rather funny – that we should first take the plank of wood out of our own eye, so that we can then see clearly in order to take a speck of sawdust out of someone else's eye! What Jesus meant by this was that we should look at our own behaviour first and sort ourselves out. Only then can we help others to do the same.

And then there are some people who look at life like this:

LIFE

They live a life that is false, like a lie. Their lives are like a big colourful balloon.

Draw balloon outline.

They are all colourful and happy on the outside, but there is only emptiness and sadness on the inside. We can all be like this from time to time, making out that everything is OK when really it isn't. A lot of people are afraid to show their true feelings.

The Bible teaches that when God created us, he did so with a great big God-shaped space in our heart. He wants to fill up that space with his joy and peace. But there is something getting in the way. It's this:

Paint the word SIN inside the balloon. Ask the children if they can tell you what 'sin' means. Many children will have a good understanding of the word. Let two or three give you an answer. Acknowledge and thank them, and then explain in your own words, in a way that is relevant to the age group. As you explain about Jesus dying for our sin, etc., elongate the letter 'I' in the word sin and then use the cross-bar of the cross to cross through the letters 'S' and 'N'.

As a Christian, I find that Jesus helps me not to be selfish; he helps me not to be false; and he helps me to own up when I have got it wrong. And I never feel like an empty balloon!

There is only one way that God intends you to look at life, and that is like this:

LIFE

Life with a capital 'L'! That means doing your best and not being afraid to make the most of every opportunity. And remember – 'L' is for love, too.

I wonder how *you* look at *your* life?

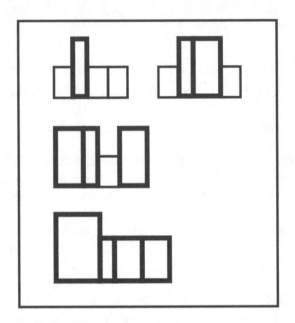

SUGGESTED SONGS:
I am listening to God (94)
2,000 years on (217)

SUGGESTED PRAYER:
Dear heavenly Father, forgive my selfish ways and give me the courage to point the finger at myself before blaming others. Also, help me not to be false and pretend to be something I'm not, but always to be honest and to live my life in the way you intended. Amen.

THREE IN ONE AND ONE IN THREE

VALUES: Choosing right; Love

BIBLE REFERENCES: Joshua 24:15; John 3:16; Romans 3:23

TEACHING POINT: Jesus can help us make the right choices.

NOTE: Instructions are provided for the use of a sketch-board – the ladder letter words are underlined.

YOU WILL NEED: Prepared sketch-board and paints, PowerPoint or OHP acetate and pens (see introductory section on ladder lettering or visit **www.canicholls.com** and **www.childrensministry.co.uk** for information on how to purchase downloads).

Today I would like to talk to you about three crosses, and how one cross can be seen in all three. The first one I would like to tell you about is the one that means WRONG. Many years ago when I was at school, I would do my sums and they would look something like this: 3 + 2 = 4

After my teacher had looked at my work, she would put this. . .

Draw in the X.

Now tell me, why do you think my teacher put a cross?

Allow the children to respond.

Even though I was only one out, do you think it was right and fair that my teacher put a cross to show that my sum was wrong? My teacher was right, because wrong is wrong, and it would be incorrect to say that it was right – that wouldn't have helped me at all, would it? Even though we don't like being told that we are wrong, it is better for us in the long run.

The next cross I would like to tell you about is CHOICE. In this country we have freedom of choice. The people who run our country, the government, are there because millions of British people decided to put them there. Every so often we have an election, when all grown-ups have the chance to say who they want to run the country. When you are old enough to vote in an election, you can go to a polling station. That is just a posh name for a hall where they collect all the votes. When you go in, you will be given a piece of paper, and on it will be the names of the people who want you to vote for them. What you have to do is. . .

Draw in the X.

. . .put a cross by the name of the person you want to win. You put a cross, not because anyone has done their sums wrong, but simply to show what your choice is.

So we have now seen how a cross can mean 'wrong', but it can also mean 'choice'. Let us look at the third meaning: LOVE.

If you wish, you can make this part personal. When I do this, I talk about when I first met my wife, and make it very funny (to the delight of the children!) by drawing a little face that is all out of proportion. If this approach does not suit your style, then just use the love letter as shown, and talk about how people who fall in love sometimes write letters to each other.

When I first met my wife, she was absolutely beautiful. She had gorgeous eyes . . . pretty hair . . . an attractive nose . . . and a lovely mouth! I just couldn't help falling in love with her! Sometimes we would write letters and cards to each other and we still send each other Christmas and birthday cards. When we wrote letters or cards, we would sign our name and then put. . .

Draw in the X.

. . .a cross. Can anyone tell me what the cross on a letter or a card stands for?

Allow the children to respond.

Yes – it stands for a kiss and it symbolises love. It's a way of saying 'I love you'.

Draw in the cross.

The last cross I would like to talk about is the cross of Jesus. It's an interesting one because it represents all the others we have been talking about. As a Christian, when I look at the cross of Jesus it reminds me that Jesus came into this world to help people who have . . . (*point to the sum*) . . . got it wrong with God. The Bible calls that 'sin'. Just like I only had to be one number out to get my sum wrong, so even one sin in my life makes me unsuitable for God's kingdom – the kingdom of heaven.

However . . . (*point to the love letter*) . . . God loves us all so much that he doesn't want us to lose out. And that is why he sent Jesus to die on the cross, to take the blame for all the wrong things we have done, and do.

This still leaves us with . . . (*point to the ballot paper*) . . . choice. One thing I have discovered about God is that he doesn't force us to do anything. He loves us so much that he will never take away our freedom. We are free to choose, and so he will never make you love him.

When I read in my Bible about the life that Jesus lived, I know three things. I know that I have done things that are *wrong* – and still do sometimes, although I try not to. I know too that God really *loves* me simply for who I am. But I also know this. I do have a *choice*: a choice either to follow Jesus or not to follow

Jesus. No one can make that choice for me, just as no one can make that choice for you. Only you can choose whether or not to follow Jesus and be friends with him.

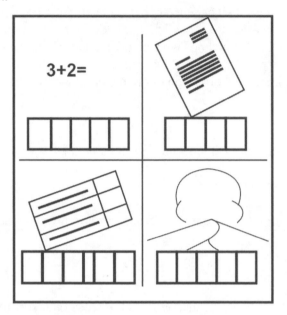

SUGGESTED SONGS:
Bind us together, Lord (18)
In the 16th verse (118)

SUGGESTED PRAYER:
Dear Father, thank you for loving me and forgiving me. Help me not to do things that I know are wrong, and help me to make the right choices in life. Amen.

THREE INTO ONE WILL GO

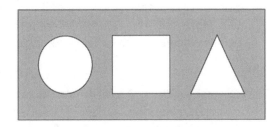

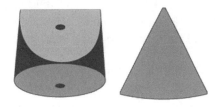

VALUE: Self-worth

BIBLE REFERENCES: John 3:16, 11:25; Philippians 4:19

TEACHING POINT: God is able to supply all our needs.

NOTES: This is a talk originally put together by the American evangelist Duane Laflin, who has kindly allowed me to use it for this book. It is visually powerful and effective, but it will require you to do a little DIY work beforehand. If you do take time to make the 'Trisquircle', I assure you that you will have a brilliant object lesson that will last for years to come.

This whole assembly hinges on the fact that the Trisquircle is a most unusual shape and not many people will have seen one.

When Duane did this talk, he had a heart-shaped piece of wood as opposed to an oblong one, but that is entirely up to your own personal taste. However, you start the assembly by having the oblong or heart-shaped piece of wood in view, making sure the Trisquircle is well out of sight.

YOU WILL NEED: One oblong or heart-shaped piece of wood with the three shapes cut out: a triangle, a square, and a circle. One Trisquircle: this is a round square triangle, which will fit into the three cut-out shapes in your piece of wood. The Trisquircle is a difficult shape to make, and you may need to seek the help of someone like a joiner who specialises in this sort of thing. (See instructions at the end of this assembly.)

There are three deep needs in the heart of every person in this room, and I would like to use this piece of wood with the shapes cut out to help me explain what they are.

The first need that I am going to talk about is the need for self-esteem. Everybody needs to feel that they are important. We all need to feel that we are of value. That's why we don't like it if people call us names or say nasty things about us, because it devalues us. I am going to use the triangular shape to represent that need: *the need for self-esteem.*

The second need that I want to talk about is the need for security. We all need to have a sense of safety. Can you imagine going home and not knowing if your home was going to be there? Or not knowing if you were going to have any tea tonight? Or not knowing if you were going to have a bed to sleep in? We all like to know that our essential needs are going to be met from day to day. We will use the square to represent that need: *the need for security.*

The third need that I would like to talk about is the need for significance. Every person needs to feel that they have a reason and a purpose for being, a reason for their existence. We will use the circle to represent that need: *the need for significance.*

I would like to ask you all a question. Is it possible to find one source or thing that can satisfy each of those needs that exist in our hearts? To answer that question, I want us to think about the shapes in my piece of wood. Is it possible to have one geometrical shape that will fit equally well into each cut-out shape here? Could a triangle shape fit into the square or the circle holes, could a square shape fit into the triangle hole, and so on?

Our lives can seem like that. One thing might satisfy one need, but not another. For example, something that will give you self-esteem will not necessarily give you security. Look at pop stars on the telly. One day people like them and are applauding them, but the next day they are getting booed off stage. So is it possible to have only one source to satisfy our needs? Is it possible to have only one shape to fit the circle, the square and the triangle?

Many people would say that it is impossible. . .

Take out the Trisquircle.

. . .but that's only because they have never seen a Trisquircle! A lot of people believe that God doesn't exist because they haven't seen him. However, the Bible teaches that one day we will see him. It also teaches that it is when we have the right relationship with God through Jesus that we find all our important needs are met. For example:

Place the Trisquircle into the triangle and say:

The Bible teaches that because of Jesus we really are important. We find that God loves us so much that he sent Jesus to die for me and for you. That makes you somebody very special and very important.

Place the Trisquircle into the square and say:

The Bible teaches that if we place our trust in God, he will supply all our needs. Philippians 4:19 says: 'God will supply all your needs according to his glorious riches in Christ.' As a Christian, I have never known God to let me down. My needs have always been met.

Place the Trisquircle into the circle and say:

The Bible teaches that with Jesus our lives have real significance. One of the things Jesus said was this: 'I am the resurrection and the life. He that believes in me, though he were dead, yet shall he live.' What that is saying is that when we put our trust in Jesus, we never have to worry about dying. We will have life that lasts for ever, and our reason for living is to love and worship God.

We have seen with this puzzle that every shape can be filled with one single object. The Bible teaches, and Christians believe, that every deep need in our hearts can be met by having a relationship with God through Jesus.

SUGGESTED SONGS:
Father, I place into your hands (44)
God is good (56)
My God shall supply all my needs (158)

SUGGESTED PRAYER:
Dear heavenly Father, help me to understand just how important I am to you. Take away any feeling of worry or insecurity, and help me to put my trust in you to supply all my daily needs. Amen.

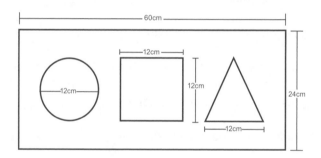

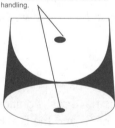

Countersunk holes either side and at the base which makes for easier handling.

Front view also showing the base.

Side view

Please note that the actual trisquircle will need to be made approximately 5cm smaller to ensure an easy fit.

pdf available

TO FLY OR NOT TO FLY?

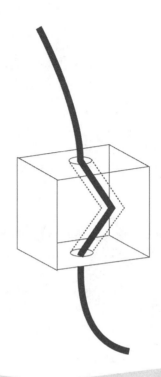

VALUE: Choosing right

BIBLE REFERENCES: Philippians 4:13; John 3:17

TEACHING POINT: By fixing our eyes on Jesus we can overcome sin.

NOTES: Once you have made the block described below you will need to practise. Hold on to one end of the rope with one hand whilst holding the other end to the floor with your foot. Keeping the rope loose, hold the block at the top of the rope and let it slide straight to the floor. Now tighten the rope slightly when the block is about halfway down so that it stops. Don't make what you are doing obvious, or it will ruin the effect. With practice you will be able to make the block fall or stop at will. This is a simple trick, but it has a powerful impact on the audience.

When I am in school and talking about sensitive issues such as sin, I will always explain that this is what the Bible teaches and what Christians believe. In this way you are keeping within the law and allowing the Holy Spirit to do what you cannot.

YOU WILL NEED: A model aeroplane. A large card with the word GRAVITY written on it. A second large card with:

SIR
ISAAC
NEWTON

written on it (it is important that the name is written as shown). A block of wood about 8 cm × 8 cm square × 5 cm thick which has a hole running from the top edge (8 cm × 5 cm) to the bottom edge, but forms a wide-angled V-shape inside the block, and a rope running through the hole. To make this, drill two holes, one from the top and one from the bottom. Both holes are drilled at slight angles and they need to meet inside the block. Thread some rope through the hole (at least 1 m in length) and tie a knot at both ends in order to stop it from coming back through. Threading the rope can be a bit fiddly, but it can be done with a little patience. (Try threading some thin wire through first, and then attaching one end of the rope to the wire.) You will see that because of the angle of the hole, when you tighten the rope it will act as a break and prevent the block from sliding. Your audience won't realise that the hole doesn't run straight through from top to bottom. Paint the block a dark colour of your choosing. If you wish, you can paint the word SIN on one face in white or a colour that stands out.

I want to ask you a question, and it's this. What is the point of Jesus? Some of you may not have heard of that name, but our dates are set by his birth. *Explain about AD and BC.* Millions of people all over the world follow Jesus – but what is the point? Let me see if I can make it easy for you to understand.

Hold up the model aeroplane as you say: How many of you have ever flown in an aeroplane? *Let the children respond, and offer one of your own experiences if you wish.*

Some people really like flying, but some people are terrified of it. Did you know that it took many years for man to learn how to fly? When man first wanted to learn, he would strap feathers to his arms and legs, go to the top of a very high building and jump off. Do you know what happened? Well, the following day the road sweepers would come round with their shovels and brooms and clear up all the mess! Before man could fly, he had to overcome one problem. Can anyone tell me what that was?

Let two or three respond. If a child gets it right, acknowledge them and continue accordingly.

Yes, that's right – gravity. Before man could fly, he had to find a power that was outside of himself in order for him to overcome the problem of gravity.

Select two children to come out, one to hold the model aeroplane and one to hold the 'GRAVITY' card.

Can anyone tell me who it was that discovered gravity?

Again, let two or three respond. If one gets it right, ask that child to come out and hold the 'SIR ISAAC NEWTON' card.

Sir Isaac Newton was sitting under a tree one day when an apple fell and hit him on the head, and he said, 'Aha! I have just discovered gravity!' Gravity had always been there – it just took someone to point it out.

The Bible teaches that there is something in all our lives that is like gravity. It has always been there, but I didn't realise it until it was pointed out to me. It weighs us down and it will stop us from living a full and happy life. Can anyone tell me what it is? Let me help you. Have you ever looked at one of those word-search books where the words are hidden amongst the other words and letters? Well, the word I am looking for is in front of you now. Can anyone see it?

Give it a little time and, if no one can respond, just highlight or encircle the vertical word 'SIN' in 'SIR ISAAC NEWTON'.

Yes, sin is like gravity. It will weigh you down. In order for us to overcome the power that sin has in our lives, we need to find a power outside of ourselves that will stop us from falling.

Here you will need your specially designed block of wood with the rope going through it. Talk about sin in your own words – what it is and the effect it can have – and each time you mention a sin, let the block slide to the floor.

Then there came a time when I realised that I needed <u>help</u> to overcome the effect that sin was having in my life.

The timing needs to be right here. As you get to the word <u>help</u>, tighten the rope slightly when the block is about half way down so that the block stops.

I found from reading the Bible that there were three things I needed to do in order for me to overcome the gravity of sin in my life. Firstly, I had to stop going my own way, and start going God's way. Secondly, I needed to say 'sorry' to God for all the bad things I had done. And thirdly, I needed to ask Jesus to be my friend.
Before that, I was just like this block of wood.

Loosen the rope slightly and let the block drop to the floor. Bring the block back to the top of the rope and just hold it ready as you continue.

But the Bible assures me, and I have found from my own personal experience, that all the time I keep my eyes fixed on Jesus, I can overcome all sorts of problems – especially the problem of <u>sin</u>.

On the word <u>sin</u>, allow the block to drop, but stop it in the centre of the rope.

SUGGESTED SONGS:
And our voices shall sing (8)
Jesus is my Saviour (126)

SUGGESTED PRAYER:
Dear Father in heaven, please forgive me when I do selfish things that upset and offend you. Thank you for sending Jesus not only to die for me, but also to teach me your ways. Help me to fix my eyes on Jesus and do those things that make you happy. Amen.

TRUST OR BUST

VALUE: Trust

BIBLE REFERENCES: Deuteronomy 31:6; Proverbs 3:5

TEACHING POINT: We can put our trust in Jesus.

NOTES: For this assembly you will need to purchase a rat-trap from a hardware shop. You may be tempted to use a mouse-trap, but that will be too small. A proper rat-trap is larger and much better from a visual point of view. It is important to practise this assembly several times in advance for it to look slick and for you to be sure it is safe!

YOU WILL NEED: Rat-trap, pencil, prepared hangman-style game on sketch-board or OHP acetate. Use part of Proverbs 3:5: 'Trust in the Lord with all your heart'. Any more words and this part of the assembly will take too long. Also, have a pie-chart which is split into six pieces. (Visit **www.canicholls.com** and **www.childrensministry.co.uk** for information on how to purchase downloads.)

Today we are going to have a game of Trust or Bust. But before we do that, I'd like you to try and work out my Bible verse. This is all of you against me.

I tend to wind the children up a bit by telling them that I have never lost this game and I don't intend to start now! The idea of course is that you don't win, but you have to play it so that it looks as though it could go either way. The excitement at the end can be electric if you gauge it right. Ask the children to put their hands up and give you a letter. If the letter is in the verse, write it in; if not, colour in a piece of the pie. If the children are getting a lot of letters correct, say something like:

Who would like an X? *Wait for a hand to go up and then say:* What a shame, there are no Xs. That's a piece of pie for me! *(Always aim that at the older children who look confident. Younger children may not understand the joke and could end up in tears!)*

On the other hand, if the children are not getting enough letters, help them out by saying:

Who would like a. . . ?

Name one of the letters that is in the verse. This, of course, can be aimed at the younger ones. Ideally, what you are trying to do is get to a position where there is one letter left and one piece of pie left.

For the last letter, always pick someone who obviously knows the answer. If, by any chance, a child purposely gives you a wrong letter in order to try and spoil the fun, answer by saying, 'I think we have had that letter,' and quickly move on to someone else.

When you are given the correct last letter, for example a D, make out that you have misheard the child and say something like: E? We have already had that one. That means I get another piece of pie!

The screams and shouts as the children correct you are amazing. Don't let this go on for too long though. Eventually 'realise' they said the letter D and put it in to a massive cheer as the children claim their victory.

OK, you beat me! So now let's play Trust or Bust. Put your hand up if you think you would trust me not to hurt you. Putting your trust in a person is sometimes difficult because people can let us down. We can also let other people down. Did you know that the Bible teaches that God has never let anyone down? There are lots of stories in the Bible where people have had to put their trust in God, and sometimes, even as a Christian, it can be very difficult. I would like to show you just how difficult, but I need a person to help me – a person who will trust me not to hurt them.

Never pick a small child to do this. Always pick one of the oldest children. Even then, always give them the option of bowing out gracefully by telling them that they don't have to do this, and that once they have seen what it is they're being asked to do, they can always change their mind. (Sometimes I have a teacher come out in a child's place.)

Produce your rat-trap.

This is a rat-trap, girls and boys. If you have a rat in your house that keeps pinching all your chocolate, you go and get one of these. I will show you how it works. You put some chocolate on there, and then set the trap.

Arm the trap and then set it off with a pencil, saying:

I guarantee that the rat will take an instant dislike to chocolate!
Now, I want you to trust me! I will re-set the trap and all you have to do is press down on that bit of the trap with your finger.

As you are talking, hold the trap towards you so that neither your audience nor your helper can see you disarm the spring. Then act as though you are setting the trap, making all the right facial expressions. Hold the trap in such a way that your thumb puts pressure on the bar and makes it look as though it is about to snap at the slightest touch. Again, ask your helper to trust you.

Here you can include all sorts of funnies like, 'Which hand do you write with? Well, use the other one!' etc. This can be a very funny and scary moment, but I assure you that you will have every person's attention and will hear the proverbial pin drop. It is a powerful object lesson.

Continue to encourage your helper by telling them that it will be OK and they really can trust you. Eventually they will slowly and gingerly put their finger in the trap and of course it doesn't go off, and there is a sigh of relief all round. Ask your helper to sit down and get everyone to give them a big round of applause as you finish by saying:

Trusting in God can sometimes be like that: very difficult. You never know what is going to happen – you just have to trust. I personally have never known Jesus to let me down.

Finish by quoting the verse Proverbs 3:5.

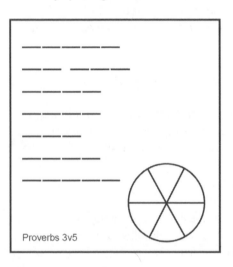

SUGGESTED SONGS:
Don't worry (37)
God knows the things we really need (59)
I once was frightened of spiders (100)

SUGGESTED PRAYER
Dear Father in heaven, please forgive me for the times I have let other people down, and help me to forgive others when they have done the same to me. Also, help me to know and understand that I can always put my trust in you and that you will never let anyone down. Amen.

WHAT ARE YOU LIKE?

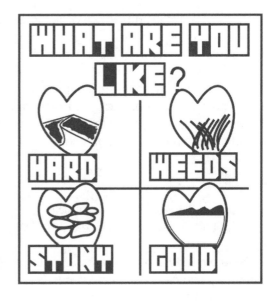

VALUES: Choosing right

BIBLE REFERENCE: Matthew 13:1–23

TEACHING POINT: Making the right response to God.

NOTES: Instructions are provided for the use of a sketch-board – the ladder letter words are underlined.

YOU WILL NEED: Four balloons of different colours, one with the end cut off; prepared sketch-board and paints, PowerPoint or OHP acetate and pens (see introductory section on ladder lettering or visit **www.canicholls.com** and **www.childrensministry.co.uk** for information on how to purchase downloads).

Today I am going to talk about the most important person in this room. I will put their name in here: <u>YOU</u>. And then I'm going to ask a question: <u>WHAT ARE (YOU) LIKE?</u>

Do you like listening to stories? Jesus loved telling stories to people. He would often use stories to explain things to them, and he would often talk in parables. Can anyone tell me what a parable is? *Let two or three have a guess, and then explain.*

Well, one day Jesus was talking to a large crowd and he said, 'A farmer went out to sow some seed.' Today, children, farmers have big tractors to help them, but in those days they had to sow the seed by hand. They would get handfuls of it and throw it and it would go everywhere.

Draw in path.

Jesus continued, 'Some seed fell on the path, which was very <u>HARD</u>, and the birds of the air saw it and pecked it up.' What Jesus was saying was this.

Bring out the balloon with the end cut off. Try to blow the balloon up. Obviously you can't because the end is missing but, as you try, it will make a funny rasping sound and the children will laugh. After two or three attempts, discard the balloon.

In the story, the seed represents the word of God – the things God wants us to know and to do – and the ground where the seed falls is like people's hearts. Some people's hearts are like that path – very hard – and no matter how much you tell them about God's love, they just don't want to know. It's like trying to blow up a balloon with no end – it's just impossible. Also, the little they do remember of what you told them, the devil steals away before it has had a chance to do any good – just like those birds ate the seed.

Can you sometimes be like that – hard-hearted and couldn't care less? Jesus taught that we should love others as much as we love ourselves.

Draw in stones.

Jesus then went on to say, 'Some seed fell on <u>STONY</u> ground where there was not much soil. It started to grow quickly, but it had no moisture and no roots. When the sun came out, the plants were scorched and they withered and died because they had no roots.' What Jesus was saying was this.

Blow up the second balloon. Do not tie it, but just hold it as you continue.

When some people hear about God, about how much he loves them and how much he wants them to care for others and follow his ways, at first they think it's wonderful. They start to learn about the things of God, but as soon as things get difficult. . .

Let the balloon go (it will fly all over the place, which the children will find funny, but it makes the point in a visual way).

. . .they give up.

Draw in weeds.

Jesus then went on to say, 'Some seed fell amongst thorns and <u>WEEDS</u>. It started to grow, but the thorns and weeds grew up around it and choked it.' What Jesus was saying was this.

Blow up the third balloon. Do not tie it, but just hold it as you continue.

When some people hear about God, about how much he loves them and how much he wants them to care for others and follow his ways, they think it sounds wonderful. They start learning about the things of God and they start to grow and live the way God wants them to. But then the things of this world, like money and possessions, take over and. . .

Let the air out of the balloon slowly so that it makes a high-pitched whining sound.

. . . they slowly give up.

Draw in good soil.

Jesus then went on to say, 'Some seed fell on <u>GOOD</u> soil and produced a crop a hundred times more.' What Jesus was saying was this.

Blow up the fourth balloon and tie it. (Optional extra: there is a trick you can purchase called 'Needle through a Balloon', which enables you to put the needle through the balloon without bursting it.)

When some people hear about God, about how much he loves them and how much he wants them to care for others and follow his ways, they think it's wonderful. They start to learn about the things of God and they start to grow and live the way God wants them to. When things get difficult, they don't give up. They just keep on growing in the ways of God, and they go on to tell lots of other people about how much God loves them.

I wonder which balloon best represents you?

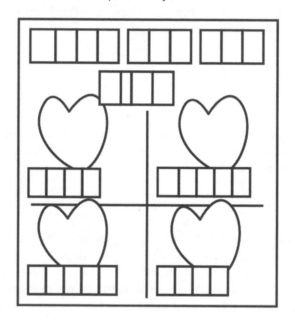

SUGGESTED SONGS:
Abba Father (4)
Colours of day (24)
I can do all things (97)

SUGGESTED PRAYER:
Dear Father in heaven, I want to be yours and yours alone. Please don't ever let my heart grow cold or hard towards your word. Help me to hear you when you speak to me, and to respond in the right way. Amen.

WHAT IS A CHRISTIAN?

VALUE: Saying sorry

BIBLE REFERENCES: Romans 3:23; John 6:37; 1 John 1:7

TEACHING POINT: A Christian is a person who has their sin forgiven by God.

YOU WILL NEED: Blue, yellow, green and red Colour Filter Gel Sheets (these are sheets of coloured, heat-resistant acetate that are used to colour stage lights in a theatre. They can be purchased from a theatrical lighting specialist. If you have Internet access, there will be many companies to choose from. One is: **www.stagebeat.co.uk**); five sheets of A3 card; a red marker pen.

Cut out an identical heart shape in the centre of four of the sheets of card. Attach the blue gel sheet to one, the green to another, the yellow to another and the red to the fourth. Draw a black outline of the heart shape on the fifth sheet of card. Inside the outline write the word SIN with the red marker pen.

(Please note that this will also work using an OHP, but you will need to reduce the card size to A4 and substitute a piece of clear acetate for the blank card.)

I would like to start by asking you a question. The question is: What is a Christian? I would like to try and answer that question using this piece of card.

Hold up the card with the outline of a heart and the word SIN.

Girls and boys, can anyone tell me what this word means? It's a word that we sometimes hear people say, and the Bible has a lot to say about it as well. A lot of people think that sin is when we do naughty things. In actual fact, naughty things – like thinking bad thoughts, and saying bad words, and doing bad deeds – are all the *result* of sin. Because sin really means going our own way instead of going God's way – turning our back on God and saying in our heart, 'I'm not interested in what God wants, I'm only interested in what *I* want!' Notice that the middle letter of the word 'sin' is the letter 'I'.

The Bible teaches that everybody in the world has sinned. We all fail to achieve God's standard, which is to be perfect. Of course, because God's standard is perfect, it is impossible for anyone to reach it. It would mean that you would have to be really, really good every minute of every day for your whole life! But sin stops us from being able to know God, and this makes God really sad because, the Bible tells us, he created us to worship him and have a relationship, or be friends, with him. I have found, though, that by becoming a Christian I *am* able to have a relationship with God. So how is this possible?

Some people may think that doing good things, like helping other people, can make us right with God.

Place the blue heart over the heart with the word SIN.

Although God wants us to help other people, doing that does not take away the sin that is already in our heart. It might make us feel good about ourselves for a while. But when God looks at our heart, he is still able to see our sin. It is like a stain, or dirty mark, that won't go away. So just being a good person does not make you a Christian.

What about believing in God?

Place the green heart over the heart with the word SIN.

Some people think they are Christians because they believe in God. But the devil believes in God, and he's not a Christian! I believe that my next-door neighbour exists, but that does not make me a member of his family. Believing in something does not make you part of it. So simply believing in God does not make you a member of God's family. Belief is not enough. It does not take away my sin that separates me from God.

What about going to church – does that make a person a Christian?

Place the yellow heart over the heart with the word SIN.

Some people would say they are Christians because they love going to church on Sunday. It's true that many people love going to church, but that does not make them Christians. If you had a friend who loved tomatoes, he could stand all day long in a greenhouse, and I guarantee that he would never turn into a tomato! I could stand in this school all year long, but that alone would not make me educated. I could stand in a church building all my life, but it would never remove the stain of sin from my heart.

So what is the answer to my question 'What is a Christian?' How do we remove that stain of sin from our heart? The Bible teaches that one of the first things a person needs to do is admit they have a problem. God never lies and can't listen to people who tell lies, and so one of the first things you have to be if you want to be a member of God's family, is truthful.

The second thing we need to do is ask God's forgiveness for all the wrong things we have done, and then we must try to stop going our own way and start going God's way instead. The Bible teaches that God promises he will never turn anyone away who turns to him.

The third thing we need to do is believe with all our heart that when Jesus died on the cross, he took the punishment for all the bad things we have done in the past, and all the bad things we may do in the future. And then we need to ask Jesus to be our friend and to come and live in our heart.

Place the red heart over the heart with the word SIN. The word SIN will be filtered out so that it can no longer be seen.

If we do this, the Bible teaches that when God looks at our heart, he will no longer see our sin – instead, he will see Jesus living in us. You can look at it like this: rather as soap and water washes away dirt from our body, so the blood that Jesus shed for us on the cross washes away sin from our heart.

So what is a Christian? A Christian is a person who has had their sin forgiven by God, and has Jesus living in their heart.

SUGGESTED SONGS:
Abba Father (4)
Seek ye first (182)

SUGGESTED PRAYER:
Dear Father, please forgive me when I sin by going my own way. Give me the strength and the courage always to be truthful and do what is right. Thank you for making it possible for me to be friends with Jesus. Amen.

WHAT IS THE ANSWER?

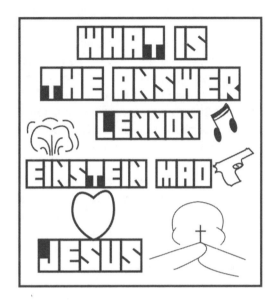

VALUES: Love; Peace

BIBLE REFERENCES: Philippians 4:6–7; John 14:6

TEACHING POINT: True and lasting peace and happiness come from God.

NOTES: This assembly is more appropriate for older children. Instructions are provided for the use of a sketch-board – the ladder letter words are underlined.

YOU WILL NEED: Prepared sketch-board and paints, PowerPoint or OHP acetate and pens (see introductory section on ladder lettering or visit **www.canicholls.com** and **www.childrensministry.co.uk** for information on how to purchase downloads).

Let's start by asking a big question: <u>WHAT IS THE ANSWER</u>?

This is a question that many young people ask as they grow up and start to think about their life and wonder how things are going to work out for them. How can they find *peace of heart and peace of mind*? I don't know anyone who doesn't want to be happy, do you?

We often look at famous people and think they can show us how to be happy and successful. Sometimes it's people from history who influence us. For example, let me put a name up here: <u>LENNON</u>.

In the 1960s there was a famous singer and songwriter called John Lennon. He was in a pop group called The Beatles. Now, The Beatles certainly influenced the music world. John Lennon and Paul McCartney wrote many songs together, songs that are still played today. *(You may want to mention some of them that the children might know.)* John Lennon wrote a song called 'Give Peace a Chance'. He wanted to stop wars and fighting and help the world become more peaceful through his music. There are many singer/songwriters who want to have an effect on the world with. . .

Draw the music symbol.

. . .their music. Talented people have been writing and singing songs about peace for as long as I can remember, but I have never known it make much difference.

Lots of people think science will help us find happiness and peace. They expect scientists to come up with answers to the questions like, 'How can we all live longer?' Or, when we get older, 'How can we look younger?'

There was a very famous scientist called <u>EINSTEIN</u>. Einstein is one of the greatest names in the world of science. All the scientists today will have read about this man and been influenced by his ideas. Science is really interesting and it has helped make some things better in our world – especially in the area of medicine. But it has never brought peace. In the hands of the wrong people it can cause us serious problems. Science has given us things like nuclear power which can be used for good things like electricity, but which can also be used for. . .

Draw a mushroom cloud.

. . .weapons of mass destruction.

Talking of destruction, you also have people like <u>MAO</u>. Mao Tse Tung, also known as Chairman Mao, was a Chinese leader who died in the 1970s. He was a revolutionary, which means he wanted to change society – not just to make little changes, but to turn everything upside-down. And of course he wanted to be in charge of everything himself. Mao persuaded his followers that the answer to their problems was in. . .

Draw a gun.

. . .scaring and hurting people by violence and war. There are people in the world who are still doing this today. But no lasting peace has ever been brought about by violence. It is widely believed that tens of millions of people died as a result of Mao's ideas.

So what *is* the answer? How do we find peace of heart and peace of mind?

The Bible says we can find the answer within us! But how? I would like to put up the name of another revolutionary: JESUS. Jesus has changed the hearts of millions of people, not with songs or science or war, but with. . .

Draw a heart.

. . .*love.* Two thousand years ago, God sent his Son, Jesus, into the world to show us just how much he loves us. Jesus did this. . .

Draw a cross.

. . .by dying on the cross for all the bad things we have done in the past and still do today – everything that separates us from God, the one and only source of everlasting peace and happiness.

So how can we experience this peace? Jesus said, 'I am the way, the truth and the life. No one comes to the Father except by me.' This means that everyone who asks Jesus to be their friend, and decides to live their life in the way he wants them to – which is basically to love God and love other people – will find they have the peace of God in their heart. Not a peace that is here today and gone tomorrow, but a peace that will last for ever, no matter what happens.

The Bible says: 'Do not be anxious about anything, but in everything, by prayer and petition – which means 'asking' – with thanksgiving, present your requests to God. And the peace of God, which transcends all understanding, will guard your hearts and your minds in Christ Jesus.'

WHO LIKES SWEETS?

TOP
QUALITY
CAT FOOD

VALUES: Respect; Tolerance

BIBLE REFERENCE: 1 Samuel 16:7

TEACHING POINT: Man looks at the outward appearance, but God looks at the heart.

NOTES: Carefully take off the cat food label and stick it onto the tin of cherry pie filling. Most tins these days have a ring-pull in order to open it, but that can sometimes snap off and leave you stranded so I recommend you always carry a tin opener with you, just in case. Put the chocolate bar, tin of cherry pie filling with the cat food label, the other grocery items, the tin opener and a spoon in the bag.

YOU WILL NEED: A shopping bag, a KitKat chocolate bar, a tin of cherry pie filling, a tin of Kit-e-kat cat food (make sure the two tins are the same size), a tin opener, a spoon, several other tins, boxes or packets of grocery items.

Today, children, I have been shopping. Look at all the things I've bought!

Hold up your shopping bag. Show some of the items – at this stage include the KitKat but do not bring out the tin with the swapped label.

Have you ever thought about all the different labels there are? Did you know that companies spend thousands of pounds on having a label designed? Why do you think that might be?

Let two or three children respond, and always thank them for answering your question.

Do you realise that we are just like those companies in many ways? We might not be a bag of dog biscuits, but we still spend money on dressing up. We like to wear the latest designer clothes so that we look good. When we look good, it makes us feel good. We like to look cool, don't we? Even if we're not wearing designer clothes, we still label ourselves. A school uniform is like a label. It lets other people know that you are a member of this school. In a way, when we label ourselves, whether at school or when we go out, we are making a statement that says, 'This is who I am.'

Let's move on. Who likes sweets and chocolate? *(Lots of hands will go up!)*

So do I. Well, I am feeling very generous today so I think I will give away the KitKat. Who would like to come and eat it?

Again, lots of hands will go up. Pick an older child who looks quite confident. It is wise to advise the head teacher what is going to happen beforehand. This can also help you ensure that the child you select doesn't have any food allergies. Ask the child to come out and, when they are standing next to you, bring out the tin labelled 'Kit-e-kat'. The look on everyone's face will be an absolute picture – especially the child who now thinks he/she has got to eat from a tin of cat food!

Don't worry, it's got all the best ingredients. *(Read some of the ingredients from the label.)*

It says it will give you plenty of bounce and put a spring in your tail! Wonderful!

While everyone is laughing, you need to whisper to the child in order to reassure him/her that it is not cat food and that it will be safe – and really nice –

to eat. If you need to repeat the whisper, get the children to make more noise by saying something like, 'Do you think he/she should give it a go?' The children will all be shouting 'Yes!' or 'No!' Once you have convinced the child that it will be OK to eat, continue:

Look, I have come prepared. I even have a tin opener if the ring-pull doesn't work. And I have a spoon. You are really going to enjoy this!

Undo the can and offer the child a couple of spoonfuls. The 'yuk!'-type reactions coming from those watching are always absolutely priceless as the child eats what the onlookers think is cat food. The faces of some of the teachers can be a picture too.

Reveal that it is really a tin of cherry pie filling. Thank the child for helping you, and then give him/her the KitKat chocolate bar as a thank you. Get everyone to give the child a big round of applause as he/she goes back and sits down.

Well, that was fun, wasn't it? But there is a serious truth we can learn from this. You were all looking at the *outside* of the tin. You couldn't see what was *inside* and, because of that, you were fooled. We can do exactly the same with other people, and we can do exactly the same with ourselves.

We sometimes meet someone and make a judgement about that person based on what they look like. Before we have got to know them, we can make up our mind as to whether or not we like them.

Also, we sometimes dress up and make ourselves look good on the outside, so that no one will know that deep down inside we are feeling sad, depressed and even empty. Did you know that the Bible teaches that God knows exactly what is going on inside us, and that he is never fooled? The Bible says that 'Man looks at the outward appearance, but God looks at the heart.'

I wonder, what does God see when he looks at your heart? Does he see a happy person, a sad person or a worried person? Whatever you really feel like deep down inside, I've learnt from reading the Bible that God never says 'Yuk!' or 'What a hopeless case!' He loves you very much, and wants to help you and stick with you all through the good times *and* the difficult times in your life.

Optional gospel ending:
I can't see into your heart, but one thing I do know is this. The Bible teaches that God does see a lot of sin in our hearts, that is, all the naughty behaviour – bad

thoughts, bad words and bad deeds. It makes God very sad, because sin separates us from him.

You can continue by talking about God sending Jesus to die for our sin, and how we can be friends with God by becoming friends with Jesus.

SUGGESTED SONGS:
God gave me ears (55)
I'm made in the image of God (114)

SUGGESTED PRAYER:
Dear Father in heaven, please forgive me when I have judged others by their outward appearance, and give me the ability to judge myself first. Enable me to see other people as you see them, and to change those things about me that need to be changed. Amen.

WHO LIVES HERE?

VALUES: Friendship; Love; Thoughtfulness

BIBLE REFERENCES: Luke 10:27; Ephesians 4:26; Philippians 4:6; 1 Corinthians 6:19; John 3:16

TEACHING POINT: God wants to live in our lives.

NOTES: I have found this to be a very useful talk to have under my belt if I find myself short of preparation time. There is hardly any advanced preparation as it is all done using pictures that can be quickly and easily drawn during the presentation. Instructions are provided for the use of a sketch-board – the ladder letter words are underlined. The only words required are WHO LIVES HERE? and you could just write them up in regular text at the start of the assembly. If you prefer doing a PowerPoint presentation, you can have the pictures stored on your laptop and project each one as you speak about it.

If handled well, this simple talk makes for a powerful assembly, but please be aware of political correctness.

YOU WILL NEED: Prepared sketch-board and paints, or OHP acetate and pens, or PowerPoint presentation (see introductory section on ladder lettering or visit **www.canicholls.com** and **www.childrensministry.co.uk** for information on how to purchase downloads).

Draw in the heading <u>WHO LIVES HERE?</u>

Draw an igloo, and ask the children what it is.

Yes, it's an igloo. Can anybody tell me who would live in a place like this?

Some children may use the name 'Eskimo'. When acknowledging their answer, it would be wise to explain that the correct name is 'Inuit'. Otherwise, in this age of political correctness, you could find yourself being hauled over the coals by the head teacher!

Yes, that's right, an Eskimo – or, to use the proper name, an Inuit. The Inuits are skilful people and they are able to cut blocks of ice to exactly the right shape to make an igloo. So tell me, would that be in a hot country or a cold country?

Allow the children to answer.

Yes, a cold country. And with all that ice, it reminds me of people who can be very cold. What do you think I mean by that?

Allow two or three to give you an answer, and then talk about what it means to be cold-hearted and that God does not want us to be like that. Go on to explain that God wants us to love others as we love ourselves.

Draw a tepee or wigwam. As you are drawing, ask the children to guess what it is.

Yes, it's a wigwam or tepee. Can anybody tell me who would have lived in a place like this?

Allow the children to answer. You may well get the reply 'Red Indian', and when acknowledging the children's answers it will again be to your advantage to refer to the correct name.

Yes, you're right, a Native American Indian would have lived in one of these. Now, is America a hot country or a cold country?

Allow the children to answer.

Well, America is a big country, and so there are places where at certain times of the year it can be very cold, but there are also places where it can be extremely hot. This reminds me of people who can not only be cold-hearted, but also hot-tempered. Do you ever get angry and lose your temper? We all do from time to time, but some people can lose their temper over the slightest little thing. And when we get angry we can, if we are not careful, do some really silly things. The Bible has something very important to teach about getting angry. It says that *we shouldn't let the sun go down on our anger.* What do you think that means?

Allow two or three to give you an answer.

If you fall out with one of your friends today, it's far better for both you and your friend if you can sort it out quickly and make up again before the end of the day. If you don't, you will go home feeling all bad inside and, as I was saying, you might do something really silly and end up with an even worse situation.
Let's move on.

Draw a traditional gypsy-type caravan. As you are drawing, ask the children to guess what it is.

Yes, an old-fashioned caravan. Can anybody tell me who might live in a place like this?

Allow some children to answer, and pick up on the word 'Gypsy'. (It's amazing that even though you don't often see this style of caravan today, children are still able to make the association.)

One of the ways that Gypsies, or Romanies, would earn money – and some still do – is by telling people's fortunes.

For this part of the talk I refer to an old gypsy caravan that I saw with a sign outside saying: 'Have your fortune told!' You may even have a personal experience that you are able to share – but it is obviously wise not to say anything that might encourage children to want to go down this road.

It's amazing how many people are worried about their future. They spend money on magazines in order to read their horoscope every week. Or they go to a person who calls themselves a fortune-teller, to try and find out what their future holds. They may come away with all sorts of information about tall dark handsome strangers and so on – but can they rely on that information being true? The great thing I have found as a Christian is that I can trust God with my future. The Bible teaches that we are not to be anxious about anything. It teaches that we can pray about every single thing that concerns us, and trust God to take care of it.

Right, what about this one? I don't suppose anyone can tell me who would live in a place like this!

Draw a church, and once again ask the children to guess what it is you are drawing.

Who would live in a place like this?

Allow some children to answer. What you are wanting here is for one or two children to say that God or Jesus would live in a church. Even though this is wrong, thank the children and explain that although the answer is not correct, they have been very helpful. Then go on to say:

It's amazing how many people believe that God or Jesus lives in a church. People go into a church building to worship God – but God doesn't live there. Let me show you where, according to the Bible, God would like to live.

Draw a heart shape.

The Bible teaches that God wants to live in our hearts, but that there is something preventing him from doing that. I wonder if anyone can tell me what that something might be?

When you ask a question that you know the children may find difficult to answer, reassure them that it doesn't matter if they get it wrong, and encourage them to have a go – always, of course, thanking them for their help. It is quite possible that you will have some children who are part of a church who will know the answer.

Yes, all the bad things we do – bad thoughts, bad words and bad deeds. The Bible calls it sin.

Draw a cross and go into a simple gospel message in a way that you are comfortable with and the children can relate to – remembering as always to emphasise that this is what the Bible teaches and what Christians believe.

Because Jesus is my friend, he helps me not to be cold-hearted and not to be hot-tempered. He helps me to think before I act, and not to worry about the future. He also helps me to realise that when things go wrong it isn't always other people's fault. Sometimes it's my fault. And he gives me the courage to own up and say 'sorry'.

I can only speak for myself, although I know many Christians would say the same: Jesus makes for a peaceful heart and a happy home, no matter where I may live.

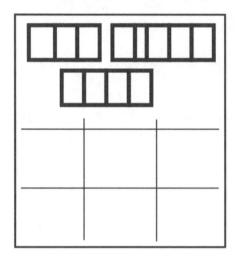

SUGGESTED SONGS:
He's got the whole wide world (86)
In the 16th verse (118)
Jesus' love is very wonderful (128)

SUGGESTED PRAYER:
Dear heavenly Father, forgive me for the times when I have lost my temper and done things that I know are wrong. Help me not to be hard-hearted or anxious, but to put my trust in you. Amen.

SCRIPTURE INDEX

Numbers refer to Assembly numbers not page numbers.

SCRIPTURE INDEX

VALUES INDEX

Numbers refer to Assembly numbers not page numbers.